The Snow Lion
and the Dragon

THE SNOW
LION AND
THE DRAGON

China, Tibet, and
the Dalai Lama

MELVYN C. GOLDSTEIN

University of California Press
Berkeley · Los Angeles · London

This book is an expansion of *China, Tibet and the United States: Reflections on the Tibet Question.* Occasional Paper, The Atlantic Council of the United States, 1995.

University of California Press
Berkeley and Los Angeles, California

University of California Press, Ltd.
London, England

First Paperback Printing 1999

Library of Congress Cataloging-in-Publication Data

Goldstein, Melvyn C.
    The snow lion and the dragon: China, Tibet, and the Dalai Lama / Melvyn C. Goldstein.
        p.   cm.
    Includes bibliographical references and index.
    ISBN 0-520-21951-1 (pbk. : alk. paper)
    1. Tibet (China)—Relations—China.   2. China—Relations—China—Tibet.   3. Bstan-'dzin-rgya-mtsho, Dalai Lama XIV, 1935–
I. Title.
DS786.G636   1997   97-2562
                                                                        CIP

Printed in the United States of America

10   09   08   07   06   05
11   10   9   8   7   6   5

The paper used in this publication meets the minimum requirements of ANSI/NISO Z39.48-1992 (R 1997)
(*Permanence of Paper*). ♾

To
CMB

Contents

DZUNGARIA

MONGOLIA

PEOPLE'S

REPUBLIC OF

CHINA

TIBET
AUTONOMOUS
REGION

Urumqi

XINJIANG

GANSU

A

QINGHAI

Xining

Lanzhou

M

D

TIBET

AUTONOMOUS

REGION

Gartok

LADAKH

Simla

INDIA

O

Nagchuka

Chamdo

SICHUAN

Chengdu

Chongqing

Shigatse

Lhasa

Yadong

Gyantse

NEPAL

KHAM

SIKKIM

Darjeeling

BHUTAN

ARUNACHAL
PRADESH

contested
border

Kunming

YUNNAN

INDIA

Preface

The Tibet Question, the long-standing conflict over the political status of Tibet in relation to China, is a conflict about nationalism—an emotion-laden debate over whether political units should directly parallel ethnic units. This question pits the right of a "people" (Tibetans) to self-determination and independence against the right of a multiethnic state (the People's Republic of China) to maintain what it sees as its historic territorial integrity.

Such nationalistic conflicts have no easy answers, for the international community has arrived at no consensus about when a people is justified in demanding self-determination or when a multiethnic state has the right to prevent secession. The current United Nations Charter illustrates the ambiguity. Whereas article 1 (section 2) states that the purpose of the UN is to ensure "friendly relations among nations based on respect for the principle of equal rights and *self-determination*," article 2 (section 7) states that "nothing contained in the present Charter shall authorize the United Nations to intervene in matters which are essentially within the domestic jurisdiction of any state."[1] Force is often the final arbiter, as when the United States went to war to settle the threat of Confederate secession.[2]

Although Tibet occupies a remote part of the world, the Tibet Question has captured the imagination and sympathy of many in America and the West and resonates throughout the American political landscape. It has also become a significant irritant in Sino-American relations. But the conflict is not well understood. Typical of nationalistic conflicts, the struggle to control territory has been matched by a struggle to control the *representations* of history and current events. Both sides (and their foreign supporters) regularly portray events in highly emotional and often disingenuous terms intended to shape international perceptions and win sympathy for their cause. History is a major battlefield, and the facts of the conflict have become obscured by an opaque veneer of political rhetoric. Interested observers are deluged with contradictory claims and countercharges that render a dispassionate and objective assessment of the conflict excruciatingly difficult, even for specialists.

The aim of this book is to peel away the layers of this veneer. In the following pages the anatomy of the Tibet Question will be examined in a balanced fashion using a *realpolitik* framework to focus on the strategies of the actors.

While issues such as cultural survival and population transfer will be discussed, this book does not focus specifically on violations of individual human rights in Tibet, such as abusing prisoners or arresting monks for peaceful political demonstrations. These rights violations exist and are deplorable, but they are not at the heart of the problem. The Tibet Question existed long before there was a People's Republic of China, and it also predates the recent Western interest in universal human rights. In fact, if there were no human rights violations in Tibet and if Tibetans could, for example, practice peaceful political dissent, the Tibet Question would be every bit as contentious as it now is. The Tibet Question is about control of a territory—about who rules it, who lives there, and who decides what goes on there.

We must also clarify the meaning of "Tibet." Ethnic Tibetan populations are distributed over an area as vast as Western Europe. They are found not only in China but also in India (Ladakh, Sikkim, northern Uttar Pradesh, and Arunachal Pradesh), Nepal, and Bhutan. Within China, the 1990 census reported 4.6 million ethnic Tibetans divided between two major regions—46 percent in the Tibet Autonomous Region (TAR) and 54 percent in the west China provinces of Qinghai, Gansu, Sichuan, and Yunnan.[3] The former area—usually referred to as "political Tibet"—is equivalent to the polity ruled by the Dalai Lamas in modern times; the latter—ethnographic Tibet—corresponds to the borderland areas occupied by various traditional Tibetan native states. Hugh Richardson, the British diplomat who served in Lhasa as an official for the colonial Indian government in the 1930s and 1940s, explained this distinction as follows:

> In "political" Tibet the Tibetan government have ruled continuously from the earliest times down to 1951. The region beyond that to the north and east [Amdo and Kham in Tibetan] . . . is its "ethnographic" extension which people of Tibetan race once inhabited exclusively and where they are still in the majority. In that wider area, "political" Tibet exercised jurisdiction only in certain places and at irregular intervals; for the most part, local lay or monastic chiefs were in control of districts of varying size. From the 18th century onwards the region was subject to sporadic Chinese infiltration.[4]

This historical differentiation between ethnographic and political Tibet has become part of the representational battleground of the Tibet Question. For example, because the Tibetan exile government has as one of its main political goals the reunification of all Tibetan areas in China into a single "Greater Tibet," it commonly uses the term "Tibet" to represent events in both ethnographic and political Tibet, fostering the appearance that "Greater Tibet" existed in the recent past. Thus, even though political Tibet was invaded in October 1950, the Tibetan exile government states that Tibet was invaded in 1949, when Chinese forces "liberated" the ethnographic Tibetan areas of Qinghai, Sichuan, and Gansu provinces.[5] Similarly, to create the impression that Tibet was part of China in the 1930s and 1940s, the Chinese government states that Tibetan delegates participated in Chinese governmental meetings, implying that they

were sent from Lhasa, whereas they were actually from ethnographic Tibet. To avoid such confusion, the term "Tibet" in this
book refers to political Tibet unless otherwise indicated.

Documenting a book on a contentious topic like modern
Tibet is difficult because much of the key information comes
from individuals who request anonymity. Nevertheless, let me
broadly describe the sources used in this book.

One important source derives from the Chinese media,
e.g., the internal broadcasts included in Foreign Broadcast
Information Service (FBIS) translations. Another source con-
sists of materials issued by Tibetans in exile (or their supporters), for example, the *Tibet Press Watch* of the International
Campaign for Tibet or the *World Tibet News*. The reports and
documents published by the London-based Tibet Information
Service provided a further source of helpful data and analyses.

In addition to these, my own extensive fieldwork in China
provided an important database. Over the past twelve years I
have conducted research in Tibet on a diverse array of topics,
including language, nomads, monasteries, modern history,
and rural development; I have spent over two full years in residence there. These research stays permitted firsthand obser-
vation of urban and rural life, and, since I speak and read
Tibetan, I was able to mix easily with Tibetans from all walks
of life without the need for guides or translators. Many
Tibetans graciously shared their views and opinions with me,
and, although their names do not appear in this book, I wish to
acknowledge my gratitude to them. Similarly, I owe a great
debt to the many officials, scholars, and intellectuals in China,
the West, and the Tibetan exile community who also discussed
important issues and events with me. Unfortunately, they too
must remain nameless. Despite this assistance, in the end responsibility for the views presented in this book are mine and
mine alone.

In a different vein, I would be remiss if I did not thank the
sponsors of my research—the United States' Committee on

Scholarly Communication with China, the National Geographic Society's Committee on Research and Exploration, the U.S. National Endowment for the Humanities, and the U.S. National Science Foundation. I also owe a great debt to Case Western Reserve University for its generous support of my research endeavors in Tibet and for facilitating my long relationship with the Tibet Academy of Social Sciences in Lhasa.

And last, but certainly not least, I want to thank my editors at the University of California Press, Sheila Levine and Laura Driussi. Their support for the project and their skill in expediting the publication of this book have been nothing short of miraculous.

The Imperial Era

Political contact between Tibet and China began in the seventh century A.D. when Tibet became unified under the rule of King Songtsen Gampo. The dynasty he created lasted for two centuries and expanded Tibet's borders to include, in the north, much of today's Xinjiang province; in the west, parts of Ladakh/Kashmir; and in the east, Amdo and Kham—parts of today's Gansu, Qinghai, Sichuan, and Yunnan provinces. Because many of the eastern and northern territories that Tibet conquered were kingdoms subordinate to China's Tang dynasty (618–907), the Chinese were well aware of the emergence of this powerful kingdom. Songtsen Gampo received a Chinese princess as a bride, and at one point in the eighth century when the Chinese stopped paying tribute to Tibet, Tibetan forces captured Changan (Xi'an), the capital of the Tang dynasty.[1] By the early ninth century, Sino-Tibetan relations had been formalized through a number of treaties that fixed the border between the two kingdoms.[2] It is clear, therefore, that Tibet was in no way subordinate to China during the imperial era. Each was a distinct and independent political entity.

During the era of the kings, Tibet transformed into a more sophisticated civilization, creating a written language based on a north Indian script and introducing Buddhism from India. The first monastery was built not far from Lhasa at Samye in about 779 A.D. The importation of Buddhism, however, produced internal conflict as the adherents of the traditional shamanistic Bon religion strongly opposed its growth and development. Ultimately, this discord led to the disintegration of the royal dynasty when the pro-Bon king was assassinated in the middle of the ninth century by a Buddhist monk angry over his persecution of Buddhism.

For the next two hundred years Tibet languished. The once great empire became a fragmented, disunified collection of autonomous local principalities. Buddhism also paid a heavy price as it was driven out of the central part of Tibet. Then, in the eleventh century, Indian Buddhist monk-teachers such as Atisha visited Tibet and sparked a vibrant revival of Buddhism. Tibetan lamas and their disciples constructed new monasteries, and these gradually developed into subsects of Tibetan Buddhism. With no centralized government, the most important of these sects, the Sakya, the Karma Kargyu, and the Drigung Kargyu, became involved in political affairs, supporting powerful lay chiefs and being supported by them in return.

In China, meanwhile, the powerful Tang dynasty collapsed in 905 A.D., and like Tibet, China experienced a period of disunity (known as the era of the Five Kingdoms, 907–960). During this period a series of buffer states occupied the frontier between China and Tibet. There is no evidence of political relations between Tibet and China. Similarly, during the three centuries of the Sung dynasty (960–1279), Tibetan-Chinese political relations were nonexistent. Chinese histories of the period barely mention Tibet.[3]

All of that changed in the thirteenth century, when a new power rose in the heart of inner Asia.

TIBET AND THE MONGOLS

The unification of the diverse Mongol tribes by Genghis Khan in the late twelfth century led to one of the greatest explosions of conquest the world has ever seen. Mongol armies swept out of the Mongolian plains and mountains and conquered immense spans of territory, including Tibet, which submitted bloodlessly to the Mongols in 1207. Tibet paid tribute to

Genghis Khan, and Mongol forces did not invade Tibet or interfere in the administration of its principalities.

The death of Genghis Khan in 1227 produced important changes. Tibetans ceased sending tribute to Mongolia and the new supreme khan, Ogedai, ordered a cavalry force under the command of his son Godan into Tibet. They advanced almost to Lhasa, looting several important monasteries and killing hundreds of monks. During this attack Godan's field commanders collected information on important religious and political leaders, and in 1244, based on their reports, Godan summoned a famous lama of the Sakya sect—Sakya Pandita—to his court in what is now Gansu. The Sakya lama arrived in 1247 and made a full submission of Tibet to the rule of the Mongols. He also gave religious instruction to Godan and his officials, and in turn was placed in charge of Tibet as viceregent. Sakya Pandita sent a long letter back to Tibet telling his countrymen that it was futile to resist the Mongols and instructing them to pay the required tribute. It also said, according to Tibetan sources:

> The Prince has told me that if we Tibetans help the Mongols in matters of religion, they in turn will support us in temporal matters. In this way, we will be able to spread our religion far and wide. The Prince is just beginning to learn to understand our religion. If I stay longer, I am certain I can spread the faith of the Buddha beyond Tibet and, thus, help my country. The Prince has allowed me to preach my religion without fear and has offered me all that I need. He tells me that it is in his hands to do good for Tibet and that it is in mine to do good for him.[4]

Thus began the curious relationship Tibetans refer to as "priest-patron" (in Tibetan, *mchod yon*). Tibet's lama provided religious instruction; performed rites, divination, and astrology; and offered the khan flattering religious titles like "protector of religion" or "religious king." The khan, in turn, protected and advanced the interests of the "priest" ("lama"). The lamas also made effective regents through whom the Mongols ruled Tibet.

Godan was succeeded by one of the greatest of the Mongol rulers, Kublai Khan. He became the supreme khan of all the Mongols in 1260 and went on to conquer China in 1279, founding the Yuan dynasty. Sakya Pandita, in the meantime, was succeeded by his nephew, Phagpa, who developed a privileged relationship with the extraordinarily powerful khan. Kublai became a great patron of Buddhism in general and of the Sakya sect in particular, making Phagpa his imperial tutor as well as the ruler of Tibet under his authority. The relationship between Kublai and Phagpa, however, was complex. In keeping with the "priest-patron" ideology, Phagpa was much more than a conquered subject put on the throne. An amazing disagreement between the two, documented in both Tibetan and Mongolian records, illustrates the great stature that Tibet's lamas held among the Mongols. When Kublai asked Phagpa to serve as his spiritual tutor, Phagpa agreed but insisted that Kublai show deference to his superior religious stature. Kublai initially refused, but eventually relented and agreed to sit on a throne lower than the lama when he was receiving private instruction, as long as the lama sat lower in all other settings.[5]

Contemporary Chinese scholars and officials consider this the period when Tibet first became part of China. Nationalistic Tibetans, by contrast, accept only that they, like China, were subjugated by the Mongols and incorporated into a Mongol empire centered in China.

The Sakya ruled in Tibet for roughly a century, until they were overthrown in 1358 by one of their governors. The Yuan dynasty was too weak to do anything but quietly accept this turn of events. In fact, just ten years later the Yuan dynasty itself was overthrown and replaced by an ethnically Chinese dynasty known as the Ming. Relations between Tibet and China continued during the Ming dynasty, but unlike their Yuan predecessors, the Ming emperors (1368–1644) exerted no administrative authority over the area. Many titles were given to leading Tibetans by the Ming emperors, but not to confer authority as with the Mongols. By conferring titles on Tibetans already in power, the Ming emperors merely recognized political reality.[6]

Then, in the seventeenth century, political events in Tibet and China saw the rise of two new powers.

THE RISE OF THE GELUK SECT IN TIBET

When Tibet was subjugated by the Mongols in the thirteenth century, the Geluk, or Yellow Hat, sect of the Dalai Lama had not yet come into existence. Tibet was dominated by several "Red Hat" Buddhist sects such as the Sakya and Kargyu. The emergence of what was later to become Tibet's greatest sect occurred only in the late fourteenth century, when a brilliant Amdo monk named Tsongkapa came to central Tibet in 1372 to seek teachings from all the great lamas of the day. A charismatic figure, he found an appalling state of moral decline in central Tibet, particularly in regard to the vow of celibacy, and he began to preach a reformist doctrine that emphasized strict monastic vows of celibacy, and scholastic study as the path for enlightenment. This marked the beginning of the Geluk, which in Tibetan means, "the system of virtue."

In 1408 Tsongkapa began the custom of convening a month-long Great Prayer Festival in the heart of Lhasa, and in 1409 he founded his own monastery—Ganden—on a ridge about twenty-seven miles east of Lhasa. As he began to write and teach, he attracted a circle of devoted disciples who spread his ideas, creating a new and vibrant Buddhist sect. To differentiate themselves from the earlier sects, the followers of Tsongkapa took to wearing yellow instead of red hats and thus have come to be known as the Yellow Hat sect. Within a short time Tsongkapa's disciples built what were to become the Geluk sect's two largest monasteries—Drepung (in 1416) and Sera (in 1419). Located just outside of Lhasa, those two monasteries became small monk-towns, housing over fifteen thousand monks by 1950. Another of Tsongkapa's famous disciples,

Gendundrup, extended the influence of the Geluk sect into southwest Tibet (Tsang) when he built the famous Tashilhunpo monastery near the town of Shigatse in 1445.

As these followers of Tsongkapa gained support among the aristocracy and their sect grew in size and importance, they engendered the suspicion and hostility of the more powerful established sects like the Karma Kargyu who were closely allied with the rulers of political Tibet, the princes of Rimpung (and following them, the Tsangpa kings). The fifteenth and early sixteenth centuries, in fact, were characterized by extensive civil and religious strife in Tibet, the Yellow Hat monks coming into recurring conflict with the Karma Kargyu and their political supporters. In 1498, for example, the Rimpung king actually forbade the Yellow Hat monks of Sera and Drepung from participating in the Great Prayer Festival begun by Tsongkapa, limiting the prayer festival to monks of the Kargyu and Sakya sects. By the early seventeenth century the sectarian conflict had worsened. In a dispute between the Geluks and the pro–Karma sect Tsangpa king, the king's troops in 1618 killed a large number of Geluk monks, occupied Sera and Drepung monasteries, and prohibited a search for the incarnation of the fourth Dalai Lama, who had recently died. The Geluk retaliated in 1633, attacking and defeating the Tsangpa king's troop garrisons around Lhasa with the help of several thousand Mongol followers. A peace agreement was negotiated, but Mongols were again playing a significant role in Tibetan internal affairs, this time as the military arm of the Dalai Lama, the main incarnate lama of the Geluk sect.

The idea of reincarnation as a method of religious succession was developed by the Karma Kargyu sect in 1193, hundreds of years before the Yellow Hat sect emerged on the scene. The idea derives from the Buddhist belief that all humans are trapped in an endless sequence of birth, death, and rebirth until they achieve nirvana (enlightenment). In the Mahayana

school of Buddhism (into which Tibetan Buddhism is sub-
sumed), some enlightened beings (*bodhisattvas*) defer their final
release from the cycle of birth and rebirth—nirvana—and return to human form to help the remaining sentient beings
progress toward enlightenment.

In the late twelfth century the great Karma lama Düsum
Khyempa used this concept to prophesy his own rebirth; and
soon after he died, his disciples discovered a child into whom
they believed he had emanated. That child was considered to
be Düsum Khyempa in a new body, so the charismatic authority and stature of the old master lama were now inherent in the
child. In a world where religious sects constantly competed for
lay patrons, the religious and political benefits of this form of
rebirth were striking, and it quickly became a general part of
the Tibetan religious landscape. Incarnate lamas developed lin-
eages, which functioned like corporations in the sense that
they came to own property and peasants and retain a legal
identity across generations. New incarnations of the initial
great lama formed an unbroken line of succession. As long as
everyone accepted the validity of the discovery process, the
powerful charisma of a holy lama could be routinized and the
focus of devotion and support continued. It is not surprising,
therefore, that the Yellow Hat sect also adopted this tradition
when one of their most important religious leaders,
Gendundrup (the founder of Tashilhunpo monastery) died in
1474. His disciples searched for and discovered his reincarnation in the body of Gendun Gyatso, a young boy who became
the second in the new incarnation lineage. When Gendun
Gyatso died in 1543, his consciousness emanated into the body
of another boy, Sonam Gyatso, who became the third in that
line of lamas.

Sonam Gyatso was an energetic proponent of the Yellow
Hat sect's ideology with strong missionary tendencies. His
fame reached the ears of a powerful Mongol ruler called Altyn

Khan who invited Sonam Gyatso to visit him. In 1578 they met in today's Qinghai province (Amdo). Sonam Gyatso impressed the khan with his spirituality and religious power, and they exchanged honorific titles in the manner of the time. The lama enhanced the stature of the khan in relation to other Mongol chiefs by giving him the title "king of religion, majestic purity," and the khan gave Sonam Gyatso the Mongolian title of *dalai,* "ocean" in Mongolian, the implication being that his knowledge or spirituality was as vast as the ocean. Thus was born the title Dalai Lama. Sonam Gyatso was the first to hold the title, but since he was the third incarnation in the Yellow Hat sect's incarnation line, he came to be known as the third Dalai Lama, with the titles of first and second Dalai Lama given posthumously to his two predecessors.

Sonam Gyatso solidified his relationship with the Mongols by spending the remaining ten years of his life in Mongolia and the nearby Kham and Amdo regions, giving teachings and making important inroads for the Yellow Hat sect. Much of this success was at the expense of the older Karma Kargyu and the pre-Buddhist Bon sects. When he died in 1588, the Geluk-Mongol tie was intensified as his reincarnation, the fourth Dalai Lama, was discovered in Mongolia in the body of the great-grandson of none other than Altyn Khan. The fourth Dalai Lama was taken to Lhasa in 1601 accompanied by an entourage of Yellow Hat lamas and nobles who had traveled to Mongolia for this purpose. They were escorted by a contingent of armed Mongol followers. The new Yellow Hat sect, therefore, came to be closely associated with the Mongols. In the seventeenth and eighteenth centuries this close religious/political relationship became a critical component of Sino-Tibetan relations.

The Mongolian fourth Dalai Lama died in 1616 and was succeeded by the fifth Dalai Lama who was discovered in central Tibet, not far from Lhasa. Sectarian strife intensified in his youth, when an ally of the Tsangpa king started to persecute

Geluk monks and institutions in Kham and talked of moving into central Tibet to attack the Geluk sect's main centers. The Geluk feared this was the beginning of a concerted effort to wipe out their sect and turned for help to their Mongol adherents in the person of Gushri Khan.

Gushri Khan was the chief of the Qoshot tribe, a branch of the Western Mongols who were based in Dzungaria, in present-day northeast Xinjiang. As a follower of the Dalai Lama he answered his lama's call for help and between 1637 and 1640 defeated the anti-Geluk forces in Amdo and Kham, resettling his whole tribe in the process in Amdo. Then, at the request of Sonam Chöpel, the chief steward (administrator) of the fifth Dalai Lama, Gushri marched into Tibet where he attacked the Tsangpa king himself at his home base in Shigatse. The Geluk sect sent its own force of supporters and monks to assist him, and in 1642 they captured Shigatse. The king of Tibet (the Tsangpa king) was executed.

Gushri Khan gave supreme authority over all of Tibet to the fifth Dalai Lama, appointing the Dalai Lama's chief steward, Sonam Chöpel, as regent to carry out the day-to-day affairs of state. The main rival of the Yellow Hat sect, the Karma Kargyu, bore the brunt of the defeat and were actively persecuted by the Geluk government. Much of their wealth and property was confiscated and many of their monasteries were forcibly converted to the Geluk sect. The Yellow Hat sect therefore quickly eclipsed all the others in size, strength, and wealth.

Using foreign troops to seize power in one's country is dangerous; it is easier to persuade them to come than induce them to go. This is what happened in Tibet. Gushri Khan did not pick up his troops and return to Amdo after winning Tibet for his lama. Instead he took the title of king of Tibet for himself and his descendants and remained in Central Tibet, spending his summers in a pasture area north of Lhasa and his winters in Lhasa. The military power behind the new

Yellow Hat government remained in his hands. The Dalai Lama and a regent administered the country, but it appears clear that they had to defer to his views to some degree.

At the time the Geluk sect was unifying Tibet under its rule, another group with central Asian origins, the Manchu, were in the final stages of conquering China. In 1644 they established a new dynasty, the Qing, which lasted until 1911. The Geluk sect and the Manchu had only cursory contact before they both came to power, but afterward, the Qing emperor invited the fifth Dalai Lama to visit Beijing and he agreed, arriving there in 1656. The Qing emperor treated the Dalai Lama with great courtesy and respect. There was nothing in this meeting to indicate political subordination on the part of the Tibetan prelate. With his Qoshot Mongol army behind him and his broad following among other Mongol tribes, some of whom were a threat to the Qing themselves, the Dalai Lama was not someone to be trifled with.

Stability in Tibet continued until the fifth Dalai Lama died in 1682. Then the weakness of reincarnation succession started a process of decline. Since the deceased lama can emanate only into someone born after his death, there is inevitably a period of fifteen to twenty years when the new incarnation-ruler is a minor, and a period of potential instability as others try to rule in his name. Sangye Gyatso, Tibet's regent at the death of the fifth Dalai Lama, dealt with this "crisis" by hiding the death from the nation. Whether motivated by fear that his position was in jeopardy or that general disturbances might arise, he pretended that the Dalai Lama had withdrawn for extended meditation and could not be disturbed. He maintained this hoax for fourteen years, ruling in the fifth Dalai Lama's name until 1696 when the secret became public.

During this period, the regent also intrigued with the powerful Dzungar Mongols, whose chief, Ganden, had been a monk at the main Geluk monasteries in Lhasa. It appears that the Tibetan regent encouraged the Dzungars (in the Dalai Lama's name) to unify all Mongols under their rule. When the Dzungars attacked the Eastern (Khalkha) Mongols and won a major victory in 1682, a new unified Mongolia seemed again possible.

One can only surmise that the regent wanted to use the might of the Dzungars to offset the military power of the Qoshot Mongols in Tibet, perhaps even to force them out of Tibet and back to Amdo. He may also have felt that the power and prestige of the Dalai Lamas would be greatly enhanced in a Mongolia united under the Dzungars, who looked to him as their main lama. But the regent was playing a high-risk game: the Dzungars were the last group strong enough to challenge the supremacy of the Qing dynasty, so siding with them meant opposing the interests of the Qing.

The Dzungar attempt to unify all Mongols, however, failed. The defeated Eastern Mongols sought the protection of the Qing emperor, who accepted their submission and, thinking that the Dzungar's spiritual leader, the fifth Dalai Lama, was still alive, asked that he use his religious authority to persuade the Dzungars to stop their invasion. Without informing the Qing emperor that the Dalai Lama was dead, the Tibetan regent sent a lama emissary to the Dzungars ostensibly to persuade them to desist in their invasion, but he appears to have conducted rites to ensure their victory. The Dzungars continued moving south toward Inner Mongolia. At this point the Qing emperor sent a large army against them and in 1696 won a major victory at the Kalulun River in Mongolia. Ganden committed suicide. The Dzungar's threat to the Qing dynasty was over, but a dangerous message had been sent to the Qing emperor regarding the importance of Tibet's lamas and the political untrustworthiness of the Tibetan regent.

Almost immediately, the Qing found an opportunity to meddle in Tibetan affairs. When Lhabsang Khan, Gushri Khan's grandson, assumed the title of king of Tibet in 1697, he set out to restore the political authority that his grandfather Gushri Khan had wielded. This placed him in direct conflict with the

Tibetan regent, who wanted no Mongol influence in his administration.

A bone of contention for Lhabsang Khan was the behavior of Tsayang Gyatso, the sixth Dalai Lama. This boy had been secretly identified as the new Dalai Lama soon after the death of the fifth Dalai Lama, but because the regent was keeping the fifth's death a secret, he announced only that this child was the incarnation of another lama. Thus, Tsayang Gyatso was not enthroned as the sixth Dalai Lama until 1697 when the news of the fifth's death became public.

The sixth Dalai Lama, however, turned out to be totally deviant in attitude and values, refusing to play the role of a celibate religious practitioner. He renounced his monastic vows and became a famous libertine, writing love poems and carousing with women at night in Lhasa. Lhabsang Khan was among those who believed that the regent was remiss in not insisting the Dalai Lama act like a true lama. Whether this demand was based on sincere conviction or simply a means to attack the regent is unclear. However, relations between the regent and Lhabsang Khan steadily worsened until 1705 when Lhabsang, supported by the Qing emperor and allied with a number of aristocratic Tibetan families, attacked the regent in Lhasa, defeating his forces. The regent was executed and Lhabsang Khan become the king of Tibet in fact as well as in title.

The emperor of China sent an envoy to Lhasa and recognized the khan as ruler of Tibet under his protection. The khan, in turn, agreed to make regular tribute payments to the Qing in return for their support. Thus Lhabsang Khan placed himself and the Tibet he now ruled in a subordinate relationship to the Qing dynasty. Lhabsang Khan also publicly announced that Tsayang Gyatso was not the true sixth Dalai Lama, and with the approval of the Qing emperor, sent him to exile in Beijing, foisting off another monk of the appropriate age as the person who should have been recognized years earlier as the real sixth Tibetan prelate. Lhabsang's military control of Tibet enabled him to impose his will, but it angered the monks and populace, who continued to consider Tsayang Gyatso as the true sixth Dalai Lama. When Tsayang Gyatso died en route to Beijing, rumors quickly arose in Tibet that he had emanated into a new body in Litang (in Kham) in accordance with a hauntingly beautiful poem he had written before his death that said,

> Lend me your wings, white crane;
> I go no farther than Litang, and thence return again.[7]

As displeasure with the situation in Lhasa rose, the monks of the three great Geluk monasteries around Lhasa turned to the Geluk's Mongol followers, the Dzungars, for aid in overthrowing Lhabsang Khan and his false Dalai Lama and installing the boy from Litang as the seventh Dalai Lama.

In 1717 seven thousand Dzungar cavalrymen entered Tibet and, with the aid of a number of Tibetan monks and laymen, quickly defeated Lhabsang Khan, who was killed in the fighting. The Dzungars appointed a new Tibetan regent, deposed the "false" sixth Dalai Lama installed by Lhabsang, arrested and executed a number of aristocrats and lamas who had been close supporters of Lhabsang Khan, and became the new rulers of Tibet. However, the Mongols soon alienated Tibetans by engaging in looting and by executing some Red Hat lamas. And critically, they failed to bring the new seventh Dalai Lama from Amdo to Tibet, as they had promised. The Qing emperor and his allies, understanding the political importance of the Dalai Lama, beat the Dzungars to the punch and placed the Litang boy under their control. Opposition to the Dzungar presence grew quickly in Lhasa.

In the meantime, two important Tibetan aristocrats—Pholhanas and Khangchennas—began to organize forces in west and southwest Tibet to oppose the Dzungars, and the Qing emperor, Kangxi, sent an army into Tibet in response to a plea for help dispatched by Lhabsang Khan before his defeat.

When this Qing army was annihilated by the Dzungars, most court officials in Beijing were opposed to further military operations in Tibet, but the emperor saw Tibet as an important buffer for western China (Sichuan, Gansu, and Yunnan) and was unwilling to allow it to remain in the control of his enemy, the Dzungars.[8] Consequently, he ordered a second, larger army into Tibet, sending the young seventh Dalai Lama with them. As the Qing troops entered Tibet from Amdo and Kham, the Tibetan forces of Pholhanas and Khangchennas also moved on Lhasa from the southwest. This time the Dzungars were defeated, and in October 1720 the Qing army entered Lhasa with the new seventh Dalai Lama. Qing troops now controlled Lhasa and Tibet.

The Qing emperor was not interested in administratively absorbing Tibet into China. His goal was to control the actions of Tibet's fractious leaders, and particularly to prevent its lamas from using their religious sway over the Mongols to harm Qing interests. In the past the Qing had tried to win the friendship and allegiance of high Tibetan lamas like the Dalai Lama through titles and gifts, but that approach had proved insufficient. Now the Qing decided to create a kind of loose protectorate over Tibet to enforce its dynastic interests. The powerful Qing dynasty would protect Tibet from external and internal conflict, leaving Tibetan leaders it approved of to rule Tibet in a manner that was not inimical to Qing interests. The structuring of this passive hegemony took the Qing the rest of the eighteenth century and forced them to send armies into Tibet on three more occasions.

The Qing made a number of important changes in the administration of Tibet. They installed the fifteen-year-old Litang boy in the Potala Palace as the seventh Dalai Lama and arrested and executed the main pro-Dzungar officials, including the Tibetan regent the Dzungars had appointed. The Qing solidified their new dominance in Tibet by building a military garrison in Lhasa and staffing it with several thousand troops.

They also eliminated the office of regent (initiated by the Qoshot Mongols in 1642), replacing it in 1721 with collective rule by four ministers (*kalön*), one of whom, Khangchennas, was appointed chairman. All four ministers were important lay Tibetan officials who had supported Lhabsang Khan and opposed the Dzungar's invasion.

Father I. Desideri, a Jesuit priest living in Lhasa at this time, prophetically wrote of this event: "After nigh twenty years of tumult and disaster this . . . Tibet . . . was thus subjugated by the emperor of China in October, 1720, and here his descendants will probably continue to reign for many centuries."[9] The religious conflict between the Geluk and Karma Kargyu sects had therefore brought Tibet under the control first of the Qoshot Mongols, then of the Dzungar Mongols, and finally of the Qing dynasty. The latter would remain the overlords of Tibet until they fell from power in China in 1911.

The 1720 Qing administrative reforms did not go well. The strategy of replacing a single all-powerful regent with a number of ministers created bitter dissension rather than a stable balance of power. In 1727 civil war erupted when three ministers assassinated the chief minister Khangchennas and tried to kill Pholhanas, a minister who supported him. Pholhanas, however, escaped the assassination plot and raised an army in southwest and west Tibet, his home area. He moved on Lhasa and defeated the other ministers, taking control of the city in July 1728.

No Qing troops were present to restore order in Lhasa because the emperor had withdrawn his garrison in 1722 after Tibet's ministers complained that it was difficult to feed several thousand troops from what was basically a feudal subsistence economy. Consequently, when he learned of the coup attempt in Tibet, the Qing emperor had to dispatch another imperial army to Lhasa (the third in a decade). This force arrived two months after Pholhanas had taken the city. With the situation calm and the ministers responsible for the coup under

Pholhanas's control, the Qing commander and Pholhanas jointly formed a judicial board that ordered the execution of the
three ministers and their families as well as a number of other
officials and lamas involved. New ministers were appointed,
but Pholhanas, now clearly the dominant figure, was confirmed
as the chief administrator of Tibet. The twenty-two-year-old
seventh Dalai Lama, however, experienced a different fate. He
was sent into exile in Kham, together with his father, who had
apparently intrigued with the fallen ministers as well as with
the Dzungars.

Administratively, the Qing imposed reforms they hoped
would stabilize the situation in Tibet. To ensure law and order,
the Qing military garrison was reestablished in Lhasa with two
thousand troops. A supporting garrison of one thousand
troops was set up in Chamdo, in eastern Tibet, to facilitate the
deployment of reinforcements. Additionally, the emperor now
decided to station two Manchu imperial residents (known as
amban) in Lhasa with orders to keep a close watch on the leaders of Tibet and oversee the garrison in Lhasa.[10] The practice of
having Qing *ambans* in Lhasa continued until 1912.

The Qing also weakened Tibet by substantially reducing its
territories in the border area between Tibet and China. In 1728
three large ethnic Tibetan areas in Kham were placed under the
jurisdiction of Sichuan and three others under the jurisdiction
of Yunnan province.[11] Amdo or Kokonor had already been
placed under the jurisdiction of Xining in 1724 after a revolt by
the Mongol khans ruling there. The emperor tried to further
fragment Tibet in 1728 by offering the Yellow Hat sect's second
greatest incarnation, the Panchen Lama, administrative control
over all of southwest (Tsang) and western Tibet. The Panchen
Lama refused this offer, but ultimately accepted control over
three large districts in Tsang. The Lhasa government, therefore,
now ruled a substantially scaled-down political entity.

The reforms of 1728 were effective, and for the next nineteen
years Tibet was internally peaceful. Pholhanas was a strong

and capable administrator who was able to operate a well-run and stable government while skillfully gaining the confidence of the *ambans* and the Qing emperor. He quickly persuaded Beijing to reduce the garrison in Lhasa to five hundred troops, and in 1735 brought the seventh Dalai Lama back from exile, although excluding him from any involvement in the administration of Tibet. The Dalai Lama was now nothing more than a spiritual figurehead. In 1739 Pholhanas was given the title of prince by the Qing emperor, becoming, in essence, the king of Tibet. The two *ambans* remained in Lhasa but had little to do with everyday administration; Pholhanas determined the course of Tibetan events. As one Chinese historian notes, Pholhanas "made all the decisions in Tibet, the *amban* being consulted merely regarding their implementation."[12]

When Pholhanas died in 1747, his son Gyurme Namgye inherited his title of prince. One hundred years after unification under the fifth Dalai Lama, Tibet was now ruled not by Dalai Lamas but by a lay aristocratic family as a Qing dependency. Gyurme Namgye's attitude toward the Qing was very different from his father's. Pholhanas had skillfully managed Sino-Tibetan relations by carefully exuding an attitude of friendship and loyalty to the Qing, securing in return the freedom to rule Tibet in accordance with its native customs and values. His son, on the other hand, sought to rid Tibet of all vestiges of Qing overlordship. He complained to the emperor Qian Long that Qing troops need not be stationed in Tibet and that the emperor's imperial commissioners, the *ambans*, were interfering in his administration and exploiting the people. Since Tibet had been peaceful and unproblematic for the previous two and a half decades, the emperor agreed to reduce the Lhasa garrison to a token one hundred troops and instructed the *ambans* in Lhasa not to interfere in Tibet's administration. He also agreed to send additional funds to cover the expenses of the *ambans* and troops, thus reducing the need for corvees (that is, taxation in the form of forced labor) to obtain goods and services. But Gyurme Namgye wanted all troops and *ambans* out of Tibet. He began to organize a secret Tibetan army of his own and, disastrously, began to intrigue with the habitual enemies of the Qing dynasty, the Dzungar Mongols.

When the *ambans* in Lhasa learned of these machinations, they invited him to their residence in Lhasa and murdered him. In response, Gyurme Namgye's followers attacked the *ambans'* residence and killed them together with their troops. Another several hundred Chinese sought refuge in the Potala under the protection of the seventh Dalai Lama and were spared. The Qing emperor, Qian Long, ordered an army to march to Tibet.

Into this political void, the seventh Dalai Lama intervened. He stopped the rioting and killing of Chinese and Manchu, appointed a lay aristocrat to operate the government, and had the leaders of the riot captured. Consequently, by the time the Qing emperor's troops reached Lhasa order had been restored under the authority of the Dalai Lama. The Qing commander publicly executed a number of Gyurme Namgye's supporters, and, as in 1723 and 1728, made changes in the political structure, this time drawing up a formal reorganization plan to permanently stabilize Tibetan politics called the "Thirteen Article Ordinance for the More Efficient Governing of Tibet." Having tried to control Tibet through a lay aristocratic family, the Qing now restored the Dalai Lama as ruler but elevated the role of the *amban* to include more direct involvement in Tibetan internal affairs. At the same time the Qing took steps to counterbalance the power of the aristocracy by adding officials recruited from the clergy to key posts. For example, a monk minister was added to the new council of ministers, and from this time the abbots and the chief managers (*chiso*) of the three great Geluk monasteries around Lhasa (Drepung, Sera, and Ganden) took part in discussions with the council ministers on important affairs.[13]

For several decades, peace reigned in Tibet, but the country was weak and disunited. When a dispute between Tibet and Nepal precipitated a Nepalese invasion in 1788, the Tibetans could not defend their country. The Nepalese looted Tashilhunpo, the monastery of the Panchen Lama, and occupied a substantial portion of southwest Tibet. The Qing emperor sent a large Chinese army into Tibet that joined Tibetan forces in 1792 to push the Nepalese out and force them to sue for peace. It was the fifth army the Qing had sent to Tibet in the eighteenth century.

The inability of the Tibetans to expel the Nepalese forces without an army from China, coupled with charges of poor leadership and organization in the Tibetan government, prompted yet another Qing reorganization of the Tibetan government, this time through a written plan called the "Twenty-Nine Regulations for Better Government in Tibet." This reform package included the selection of top incarnations (*hutuktus*) like the Dalai and Panchen Lamas through a lottery conducted in a golden urn, the aim being to prevent the selection of incarnations being manipulated to fall in politically powerful lay families.[14] It also elevated the *ambans* to equal political authority with the Dalai Lama for major administrative issues and appointments and mandated that nominations for top positions like council minister be submitted to the emperor for approval. The reforms also included regulations forbidding exploitation of peasants through the misuse of corvee labor, and prohibited the relatives of the Dalai and Panchen Lamas from holding public office during the lamas' lifetimes. Qing military garrisons staffed with Qing troops, moreover, were now established near the Nepalese border at Shigatse and Dingri.[15]

The Qing rationale for these changes was conveyed by Fu Kangan, the general in charge of the expeditionary force, in comments to the Dalai Lama at that time:

> The administration of Tibetan local affairs has never had any system to go by. All the Dalai Lama does is silent meditation and is therefore not well-informed of events taking place outside. The *kaloons* [council ministers] cheat with wild abandon in

times of peace, and in times of war they are not able to do anything [in] defense. Extensive regulations are needed so that
everyone knows what he is expected to do. In this regard His
Majesty has instructed me in great detail what to do and has ordered me and the others to deliberate on his instructions to
make sure that their execution will serve the interests of the
Tibetans for a long time to come without creating any draw-
backs. Since the Dalai Lama is grateful to His Majesty for what
he has done for Tibet, he is expected to respect the changes to be
made for better government in Tibet. If he persists in his old
ways of doing things, His Majesty will call back the resident officials and evacuate the Tibetan garrison immediately after the
withdrawal of the expeditionary army, and the Court will not
come to the help of Tibet should any emergencies arise in the future. The Dalai Lama is asked to weigh the pros and cons and
make up him [sic] mind.[16]

Fu Kangan's comments reveal Beijing's frustration with the
leaders of its Tibet dependency. Beijing had sought a peaceful
Tibet that caused it no problems, but had already found it necessary to send five armies there in less than seven decades. The
Dalai Lama agreed to the regulations and gave assurances that
his ministers would do so as well.

In the years immediately following the 1792 regulations, the
ambans exercised their greatest authority, but they made no attempt to absorb Tibet into China as a province. Tibet maintained its own language, officials, and legal system, and paid
no taxes or tribute to China. In fact, the 1792 reforms included
the creation of Tibet's first standing army, the emperor's aim
being to enable Tibet to defend itself and thus avoid having to
send troops again. In modern times the popular name of this
regiment was "Chinese trained" (or *Gyajong*).

The actual role of the *amban* in Tibet is difficult to assess.
Despite the rhetoric and rules the Qing prepared, their power
appears to have varied considerably in accordance with many
factors such as their personality and competence in relation to
that of the leaders of Tibet, and the nature of the political situ-

ation in China and Tibet at any point in time. A comment by the Qing emperor to his *amban* in Lhasa in 1792 illustrates the gap between rules and reality since 1728:

> Usually capable, competent officials are assigned to posts in the capital; those sent to Tibet have been mostly mediocrities who did practically nothing but wait for the expiration of their tenures of office so they could return to Beijing. Because of that the Dalai Lama and the *kaloons* [council ministers] were able to do whatever they wished in the administration of Tibetan affairs, ignoring the existence of these incompetent officials. That is how the Resident Official [*amban*] has been reduced to nothing more than a figurehead. From now on the administration of Tibet should be effectively supervised by the Resident Official; . . . the Dalai Lama and the kaloons shall no longer be able to monopolize it.[17]

However, as the nineteenth century unfolded, the Qing dynasty experienced pressing threats to its position as a result of internal disturbances such as the Taiping Rebellion (1848–1865) and external incursions by Western countries such as the Opium War of 1839–1842. Not surprisingly, the power of the *ambans* in Tibet waned, as did the involvement of the Qing emperors. Consequently, Tibet was able to conduct a war with the Sikhs and Ladakh in 1841–1842 and another war with the Nepalese in 1855–1856 with no involvement from China, although in the latter conflict Tibet was forced to pay Nepal an annual tribute and accept a Nepalese resident in Lhasa and extraterritoriality for Nepalese traders. Similarly, the thirteenth Dalai Lama was chosen in 1877 without recourse to the "golden urn" lottery that the Qing emperor, Qian Long, had ordered in 1792. And in 1897, two years after the thirteenth Dalai assumed political control, he stopped consulting the *amban* in the selection of top officials (in accordance with the 1792 regulations) and began appointing them directly. As Phuntso Tashi, the fourteenth Dalai Lama's brother-in-law (and a former Tibetan government official) explains, "For over

100 years Tibet's holders of political power had not been able to do that. The Manchu government was displeased with this but . . . they were unable to do anything about it."[18] By the turn of the twentieth century, therefore, the Qing hegemony over Tibet was more symbolic than real, and the Tibet Question was, in a sense, *latent*—Tibet did not explicitly try to sever its ties to Beijing: it offered nominal respect to the emperor but did not defer to the emperor's *amban* in Lhasa.

That laissez-faire arrangement was permanently transformed when a third party entered the scene and set in motion a series of events that altered the status quo dramatically.

THE BRITISH ENTER THE PICTURE

By the late nineteenth century British influence on the Indian subcontinent extended right to the border of Tibet as the string of Himalayan states and principalities fell under British influence. As early as 1861 the British colonial government in India approved an "exploratory" mission to Lhasa if permits could be obtained from China. There was considerable hope that a flourishing trade might develop between Tibet and India, with India siphoning up some of the substantial Sino-Tibetan trade in tea and manufactured goods and receiving wool, horns, skins, medicinal herbs, gold, musk, and so forth, from Tibet. At that time Tibet prohibited the importation of India tea. Britain secured China's approval for such a mission in the Chefu convention of 1876, which permitted India to send a "mission of exploration " from China to Tibet either by way of Sichuan or Gansu, or from India.[19]

In 1886 a British mission—the Macaulay mission—was assembled in Sikkim to enter Tibet. Tibetan opposition prevented its departure, but its presence prompted Tibet to send troops into a border section of Sikkim it claimed as its own territory. This led in turn to a British attack in 1888 that drove the Tibetans out of the area. As a result of the fighting, the Manchu *amban* in Lhasa went to India for discussions with the British. These talks led to the treaty of 1890 in which Britain's protectorate over Sikkim was recognized by China, and the Sikkim-Tibet border was delineated. Three years later, in 1893, a British trade treaty with China obtained Chinese acceptance of a "trade mart" at Yadong on the Tibetan side of the Sikkim-Tibet border that would be open to all British subjects for commerce. The British government also secured the right to send officials to reside in Yadong (Tibet) to oversee British trade there.

Tibet, however, was not a party to these agreements and refused to cooperate in their implementation. A stalemate ensued. Such was the situation when Lord Curzon took office as the new viceroy of India in 1899. He realized that China had no practical control over events in Tibet, so he obtained permission from London to try to initiate direct communication and relations with Lhasa. The thirteenth Dalai Lama (who had assumed power in 1895) had no interest in relations with the British, so when Curzon sent him a series of letters, he returned them unopened with the reply that the Chinese would be displeased if the Dalai Lama were to correspond with the British.[20] Unable to initiate face-to-face talks with the Tibetan government, Curzon next convinced London in 1903 to permit an expedition to enter Tibet to force negotiations. The Tibetans refused to negotiate with this expedition, so its British officers and officials led their Indian troops deeper and deeper into Tibet, ostensibly to induce negotiations. The Tibetan military attempted to block their advance, and a series of battles ensued in which the Tibetans were easily defeated, suffering losses of over a thousand troops. In the battle of Guru alone, between six hundred and seven hundred Tibetan troops were killed in a matter of minutes. No match for the invaders, the British force entered Lhasa, the capital of Tibet, on August 3, 1904. They were the first Western troops ever to conquer Tibet.

Throughout this period the Chinese government (through its *amban*) urged the thirteenth Dalai Lama to negotiate with the British expeditionary force to prevent their further advance, and then when it was about to enter Lhasa, to meet with Younghusband, its leader. But China had no control over the Dalai Lama, who ignored these admonitions and fled to exile in Mongolia, fearing he would be compelled to sign an unfavorable agreement. From Mongolia, the Dalai Lama hoped to obtain the czar's support against Britain.

To secure the withdrawal of the British troops from Lhasa, the Tibetan officials left in charge by the Dalai Lama reluctantly agreed to British terms, which were codified in an agreement known as the Anglo-Tibet Convention of 1904. Signed by only Tibet and the British head of the expeditionary force—the Manchu *amban* refused to place his signature on it—this agreement accepted Britain's protectorate over Sikkim and gave India (Britain) the right to establish trade marts with British trade officials in three Tibetan towns (Gyantse, Gartok, and Yadong). In a clause that was vague enough to exclude China as well as more obvious countries such as Russia it also forbade any other foreign power to exercise political influence in Tibet. A large indemnity of £562,500 (7.5 million rupees) was levied and British troops were to occupy a part of Tibet contiguous with Sikkim (Yadong's Chumbi Valley) until this was paid. It was also agreed that the British trade agent could visit Lhasa to discuss issues deriving from the treaty.[21] By virtue of these terms, British India virtually converted Tibet into another of its "native-state" protectorates.

News of the fighting in Tibet and the seizure of Lhasa shocked many in London who had not authorized Curzon to conquer Tibet. Britain's interests transcended those of India, and considerations of Hong Kong and Russia quickly led the British foreign office to repudiate many of the political advantages secured via the Anglo-Tibetan Convention of 1904. The large indemnity was reduced by two thirds to £168,000, and British troops were prohibited from occupying the Tibetan Chumbi Valley for more than three years. Similarly, the right of the trade agent to visit Lhasa (and influence affairs there) was also unilaterally rescinded.

Nevertheless, the final Anglo-Tibetan accord opened up Tibet to British interests. However, it also created a major diplomatic and legal problem regarding China. Because the *amban* had not signed the treaty (nor had the Chinese government approved it), unless London decided to forsake China's views and make Tibet its dependency or accept its status as an independent country, it had to secure Chinese consent to its gains. The contradiction inherent in Britain's Tibet strategy was that while Great Britain had to deal directly with the Tibetan government to achieve its ends, it had to deal with China to legitimize them.

For China, the whole affair was another humiliation suffered at the hands of the Western imperialists. From the Qing court's vantage, the Dalai Lama had blithely ignored China's orders to negotiate with the British, so the British now had troops and officials resident in Tibet. Moreover, the bilateral agreement Britain and Tibet had signed contained an ambiguous clause that barred foreign powers from political influence in Tibet. Given the way Western countries had treated China over the past half century, it was not difficult for Beijing to suspect that this was a British ploy to exclude them from Tibet.

Fortunately for China, however, London's China policy did not favor transforming Tibet into a British dependency, let alone accept it as an independent nation, and the British promptly assuaged China by entering into negotiations to obtain its acceptance of the convention Younghusband had signed with Tibet. The resultant 1906 Anglo-Chinese Convention modified the 1904 accord (without the involvement of Tibet's government), reaffirming China's legitimate authority over its dependency Tibet. The key articles in the convention said: "The Government of Great Britain engages not to annex Tibetan territory or to interfere in the administration of Tibet. The Government of China also undertakes not to permit any other foreign state to interfere with the territory or internal administration of Tibet."

And "The Concessions which are mentioned [in the 1904 convention] are denied to any state other than China."[22] Thus, at a time when China was unable to exercise real power in Tibet, Britain unilaterally reaffirmed Tibet's political subordination to China.

The next year an Anglo-Russian agreement further internationalized this situation, stating in article 2, "In conformity with the admitted principle of the suzerainty of China over Thibet, Great Britain and Russia engage not to enter into negotiations with Thibet except through the intermediary of the Chinese Government."[23]

THE CHINESE REACTION

The invasion of Tibet and the Lhasa Convention of 1904 dramatically altered Chinese policy toward Tibet. Until then, the Qing dynasty had shown no interest in directly administering or sinicizing Tibet. The British thrusts now suggested to Beijing that unless it took prompt action, its position as overlord in Tibet might be lost, and with Tibet under the British sphere of influence the English would be looking down from the Tibetan plateau on Sichuan, one of China's most important provinces. The Qing dynasty, although enfeebled and on the brink of collapse, responded with surprising vigor. Beijing got the British troops to leave Tibetan soil quickly by paying the indemnity to Britain itself and began to take a more active role in day-to-day Tibetan affairs. Britain's casual invasion of Tibet, therefore, stimulated China to protect its national interests by beginning a program of closer cultural, economic, and political integration of Tibet with the rest of China. At the same time, in the ethnographic Tibetan borderland, Zhao Erfeng initiated a major campaign that quickly converted most of the autonomous native Tibetan states into districts under Chinese magistrates. And, ominously, he launched an active attack on the position of the lamas and monasteries.

At this time the Dalai Lama was languishing in exile, spending time first in Outer Mongolia and then in the ethnic Tibetan areas of what is now Qinghai province. His overture to the Russian czar had proved futile and his position in exile was somewhat precarious since he had been "deposed" by the Chinese government in 1904 because of his flight. Although Tibetans never questioned his legitimacy as their ruler, the increased domination of affairs in Lhasa by the *ambans* after his departure made him reluctant to return to Lhasa without first achieving some accommodation with the Qing dynasty that would guarantee his control of Tibet. In 1908, therefore, he went to Beijing. Arguing that the *amban* did not faithfully transmit his views to Beijing, the Dalai Lama requested permission to petition the throne directly (i.e., to bypass the *amban* as was done before the 1792 reforms). Beijing, however, was in no mood to loosen its control over the unpredictable and independent-minded thirteenth Dalai Lama and rudely refused, although it agreed to his return to Tibet to rule. The Anglo-Chinese and Anglo-Russian conventions had reaffirmed that Tibet was a part of China, and the Qing court felt that it would be easier to control Tibet through the Dalai Lama than risk trying to replace him. But their view of his position can be seen from the humiliating new title they gave him: "loyal and submissive viceregent."[24]

Nevertheless, China did not trust the Dalai Lama to be either loyal or submissive, so unbeknownst to him took steps to ensure he followed Beijing's instructions. Zhao Erfeng, the successful special commissioner who had brutally pacified the Tibetan areas of Sichuan and Yunnan, now sent an army of several thousand troops from Sichuan province to ensure that the Dalai Lama remained compliant. As the thirteenth Dalai Lama arrived in Lhasa in late December 1909, five years after he had fled from the Younghusband expedition, he learned that this Chinese army was on its way. The Dalai Lama, in desperation, sent the following poignant appeal to Britain:

Though the Chinese and Tibetans are of one family, yet the Chinese officer Chao [Zhao] and the Amban Lien are plotting together against us, and have not sent true copies of our protests to the Chinese Emperor, but have altered them to suit their own evil purposes. They are sending troops into Tibet and wish to abolish our religion. Please telegraph to the Chinese Emperor and request him to stop the troops now on their way. We are very anxious and beg the Powers to intervene and cause the withdrawal of the Chinese troops.[25]

And to the Chinese he wrote:

We, the oppressed Tibetans, send you this message. Though in outward appearance all is well, yet within big worms are eating little worms. We have acted frankly, but yet they steal our hearts. Troops have been sent into Tibet, thus causing great alarm. We have already sent a messenger to Calcutta to telegraph everything in detail. Please recall the Chinese officer and troops who recently arrived in Kam. If you do not do so, there will be trouble.[26]

No one intervened, so as that army entered Lhasa in February 1910, the Dalai Lama again fled into exile, this time south to his former enemies in British India.

China again deposed the Dalai Lama and stepped up its efforts to expand its real control in Tibet, its officials assuming more direct command of administration. A Chinese postal service was established and Tibet's first stamps were produced (in Chinese and Tibetan script). Tibet seemed set on a trajectory that would have ended in Tibet's incorporation into China proper. This process, however, was abruptly halted when the Qing dynasty was overthrown in China in 1911.

To ethnic Chinese, the Qing emperors were foreigners who had destroyed China's greatness and relegated it to the pathetic status of "sick man of Asia." From the mid-nineteenth century, China had suffered one humiliation after another: its defeat in the Sino-Japanese war of 1894–1895, for example, ended in the loss of Taiwan and southern Manchuria (the

Liaoning Peninsula) to the Japanese together with the obliga-
tion to pay a huge indemnity. This was followed by the anti-
Western, anti-Christian Boxer Uprising in 1900, which ended
when a multinational Western army marched into Beijing and
imposed further humiliating concessions and yet another huge
indemnity.

Thus it was that the Chinese organized to overthrow the
alien dynasty and restore China's greatness. The revolution
began on October 10, 1911, in Wuchang, a town in western
China, when soldiers killed their commander and took over
the town. From there it spread quickly throughout the country,
and four months later on February 12, 1912, the six-year-old
Manchu emperor Puyi abdicated. Manchu rule in China was
over.

Interlude: De Facto Independence

THE SIMLA CONVENTION

While the Chinese army of 1910 occupied Tibet, the thirteenth Dalai Lama lived in Darjeeling, India, contemplating the circumstances that had allowed Lhasa to be twice conquered within six years. During this time he developed a close friendship with Sir Charles Bell, the government of India's political officer in Sikkim, and learned a great deal about modern politics, seeing firsthand how an efficient and dedicated bureaucracy and army could rule a vast country. The beginnings of a new vision of Tibet formed.

The fall of the Qing dynasty was a stroke of good fortune that the thirteenth Dalai Lama immediately capitalized on. From exile in India he organized a military force to regain his power, and with the help of Nepalese mediation in Lhasa, soon succeeded in expelling *all* Chinese officials and troops from Tibet. The thirteenth Dalai Lama triumphantly returned to Lhasa in 1913. Yuan Shikai, the provisional president of the new Chinese government that succeeded the Qing, sent the Dalai Lama the following "reinstatement" telegram:

> Now that the Republic has been firmly established and the Five Races [Han, Tibetan, Manchu, Mongol, Muslim] deeply united into one family, the Dalai Lama is naturally moved with a feeling of deep attachment to the mother country. Under the circumstances, his former errors should be overlooked, and his

Title of Loyal and Submissive Vice-Regent, Great, Good, and Self-Existent Buddha is hereby restored to him, in the hope that he may prove a support to the Yellow Church and a help to the Republic.[1]

The Dalai Lama replied that he had not asked for his former rank from the Chinese government and that he "intended to exercise both temporal and ecclesiastic rule in Tibet."[2] Many interpret this and a proclamation he issued twenty-two days after he returned as the equivalent of a declaration of independence.

The Tibet Question, however, was far from settled since the new Chinese republican government took the position that the non-Chinese territories the Manchu emperors had subjugated —including Tibet—were part of their republic. Sun Yatsen, the "father of the revolution," for example, was extremely nationalistic and had called for the creation of a strong Chinese state that would expel the Japanese from Manchuria, the Russians from Mongolia, and *the British from Tibet*.[3] One of the fundamental nationalistic goals of the Chinese revolution, therefore, was to restore China to its former greatness, and regaining control of Tibet took on great symbolic significance. Thus, on April 12, 1912, the new Chinese republic headed by Yuan Shikai issued an edict that declared Tibet, Mongolia, and Xinjiang on equal footing with the provinces of China proper and as integral parts of the republic. Seats were set aside for Tibetans in the National Assembly and a five-colored flag was created, the black band representing Tibet.[4] The Tibet Question in its modern incarnation had been born.

Given the conflicting national aspirations, Tibet clearly had to reach some accommodation with China regarding its political status or be prepared to defend its territory and newly declared "independence." As we shall see, it turned out to be unable to do the former and unwilling to take the steps needed to do the latter. With no effective army at its disposal, Tibet sought to reach an agreement with China's new rulers and received support in this from a new friend—British India. The government of British India had found China a bad neighbor during the 1905–1911 period of direct Chinese power in Tibet. Chinese officials manning the long Indo-Tibetan border seemed to the English to be using their power to foment trouble among the Indian border tribes. Britain therefore sought to prevent the recurrence of direct Chinese control by creating a buffer state in Tibet. In 1913, with the intent of achieving that end, Britain pressured the new Chinese republican government to participate in a conference with itself and Tibet in Simla, India. The Simla negotiations produced a draft convention in 1914 that set the background for the Tibet Question during the next four decades.

Tibet initially wanted the conference to declare it independent. Shatra, the Tibetan plenipotentiary, expressed this in his opening statement when he said: "Tibet and China have never been under each other and will never associate with each other in future. It is decided that Tibet is an independent State and that the precious Protector, the Dalai Lama, is the ruler of Tibet in all temporal as well as in spiritual affairs."[5] China, on the other hand, forcefully claimed the opposite in its initial Simla statement: "Tibet forms an integral part of the territory of the Republic of China, that no attempts shall be made by Tibet or by Great Britain to interrupt the continuity of this territorial integrity, and that China's rights of every description which have existed in consequence of this territorial integrity shall be respected by Tibet and recognized by Great Britain."[6]

Tibet's only hope of achieving its aim was for Great Britain to act as its champion. British strategic aims, however, were not congruent with those of Lhasa. As in 1904, London did not want to support an independent Tibet or convert Tibet into an Indian protectorate as it had done in the case of Sikkim and Bhutan. London was still unwilling to face the international criticism that support for Tibet's claim to independence would engender and was also fearful of negatively impacting British trade interests in China and Hong Kong. So Britain proposed that Tibet be accepted as a self-governing dominion nominally under China but with Chinese influence and power severely limited.

The final draft of the Simla Convention therefore declared that Tibet would be autonomous from China, but also acknowledged Chinese suzerainty over Tibet. Tibetans would administrate Tibet with its own officials in accordance with its own customs and laws, and China would not be permitted to station large numbers of troops or officials in Tibet—but China could maintain a commissioner in Lhasa and an escort of up to three hundred men. This compromise was not the independence Tibet wanted, but nonetheless did guarantee that it would retain complete control over its affairs, including the army, currency, and all other important functions. It would also legitimize an international identity for Tibet and spare it the burden of having to prepare for possible military conflict with China. Britain, of course, achieved exactly what it had sought—a harmless buffer zone along India's northern border in which its political interests were fulfilled and its commercial interests could develop.

The Tibetan and Chinese plenipotentiaries at Simla agreed to this political compromise but found it impossible to agree where to draw the boundary between political Tibet and China. At issue was ethnographic Tibet, the belt of semiautonomous ethnic Tibetan areas in eastern Tibet and western Sichuan. Tibet insisted that all ethnographic Tibet be included in its territory while China claimed its border began a mere one hundred twenty-five miles east of Lhasa. British mediation produced a number of compromises including an Inner and Outer Tibet analogous to Inner and Outer Mongolia, but in the end the new Chinese government repudiated the final border and refused to ratify the Simla Convention.

Sir Henry McMahon, the British representative, now sought permission from London to sign the convention directly with

Tibet. The foreign office, however, balked, concluding that this would be tantamount to a formal recognition of Tibetan independence. Nevertheless, since British India had clear strategic goals it needed to meet, something had to be done. In the end it devised an ingenious innovation to secure its goal. McMahon was authorized to sign a bilateral *note* with Tibet that bound each side to the terms of the *unsigned* Simla Convention. Although this was not a real treaty, British India then felt justified in pursuing its relations with Tibet in accordance with the "autonomy" stipulated in the terms of the unsigned Simla Convention, and continued to do so for the next thirty-five years. It also obtained from Tibet a vast territory east of Bhutan (today's Indian province of Arunachal Pradesh). Here we see the beginnings of what we can think of as the "bad friend syndrome"—Western powers professing friendship for Tibet but refusing to support it in its fundamental objective of political independence while actually bolstering China's claim of real ownership.

For Tibet, Simla did nothing to resolve the Tibet Question. Since China did not agree to the convention, Tibet still had no de jure status accepted by China. And the new Anglo-Tibetan note provided no guarantees that the British would militarily defend the rights specified in the Simla Convention if China sought to enforce its claim over Tibet by force. Britain was willing to accept Tibet's right to cede the vast territory of Arunachal Pradesh independent of China's wishes, but was unwilling to acknowledge that such authority validated Tibet's assertion of independence.[7]

TIBETAN ATTEMPTS TO MODERNIZE

The failure of Simla meant that Tibet had to face the possibility of future hostilities with China. This threat prompted a clique of young Tibetan aristocratic officials led by Tsarong, a favorite of the Dalai Lama, to urge modernization in Tibet, especially the creation of a strong military able to defend Tibet's interests. The thirteenth Dalai Lama agreed, and in rapid succession new troops were levied and officers and NCOs were sent for training to India and the British trade agency in the southern Tibetan town of Gyantse. At the same time, Tibet considered joining the International Postal Union, and a British schoolmaster was hired to open an English language school in Gyantse. Tibet was taking its first steps to join the modern world.

All this, however, sent shock waves through the monastic and aristocratic elites who held most of the land in Tibet in the form of feudal estates with hereditarily bound serflike peasants. Modernization was expensive, and they found themselves facing new tax levies to support the military buildup. Modernization, moreover, was also perceived by the religious leadership as an ideological threat to the dominance of Buddhism in Tibet, and thus to what they felt was the unique character of the Tibetan theocratic state. Equating modernization with Western atheism and secularism, the conservatives believed that it would diminish the power and importance of Buddhism. In their view, Tibet had coexisted with China for centuries with no adverse consequences for the domination of Buddhism (and the Geluk sect) in Tibet, so why, they questioned, was it now necessary to transform Tibet in these radical ways? Key conservative officials therefore campaigned to convince the Dalai Lama that the military officers were a threat to Buddhism and to his own power and authority. By the mid-1920s, their efforts had succeeded, and in one of the pivotal policy decisions of modern Tibetan history, the thirteenth Dalai Lama gutted the heart of the reform program by demoting the entire group of promodernization officers and closing the English school. Overnight, Tibet lost its best chance to create a modern polity capable of coordinating international support for its independent status and defending its territory.[8]

Tibet did not, however, pay an immediate price for this retreat into the past because China was deeply absorbed in internal issues and conflicts and too weak to challenge the Dalai Lama. Thus, from 1913 when the last Qing officials and troops left Tibet to the death of the thirteenth Dalai Lama in 1933, *no* Chinese officials or troops were permitted to reside in Tibet, and the Tibetan government accepted no interference from Beijing. Chinese fortunes in Tibet improved slightly after the death of the thirteenth Dalai Lama when Tibet allowed a "condolence mission" sent by the Guomindang government of Chiang Kaishek to visit Lhasa, and then permitted it to open an office to facilitate negotiations aimed at resolving the Tibet Question. These talks proved futile, but Tibet allowed the office to remain.

The Japanese invasion of China in 1937 saved Tibet from having to defend its de facto independence from China, and Tibet continued to operate without interference from Chiang Kaishek. China did not, however, abandon its claims over Tibet. To the contrary, it effectively reinforced its position throughout the world (and in China itself) with a propaganda campaign that actively sought to create the impression that Tibet was in fact a part of China. Tibet, with virtually no officials who understood the West or spoke English, blithely ignored this ominous development, much as it had earlier closed its eyes to reality and returned British governmental correspondence unopened.

Chinese Communist Rule: The Mao Era

Victory in World War II did not enable China to address the Tibet Question since full-blown civil war broke out between the government of Chiang Kaishek and the Chinese Communist party led by Mao Zedong. The Chinese Communists emerged victorious four years later, and on October 1, 1949, Mao Zedong inaugurated the People's Republic of China (PRC).

Settlement of the Tibetan Question at this time was no closer than it had been at the fall of the Qing dynasty. Tibet was still operating as a de facto independent polity in all ways, although it was militarily weak and internally disunified due to a 1947 outbreak of bitter fighting between Sera monastery and the government over the regency of the fourteenth Dalai Lama. Tibet had also failed to secure international support for its claim to independence. Britain and India (and later the United States) dealt directly with Tibet as if it were an independent state, but continued to acknowledge de jure Chinese suzerainty over Tibet. That is, they considered Tibet a part of China. Much of the current confusion over Tibet's previous political status derives from this Western double standard.

One example of this occurred in 1943 when the United States wanted to send two OSS (Office of Strategic Services, the precursor of the CIA) officers to Tibet to travel overland to China and assess the potential for construction of roads and airfields. The United States asked their close ally Chiang Kaishek to arrange this, but since China exercised no control over Tibet, the Tibetan government turned down his request.

The United States was then forced to ask the British (who had a representative in Lhasa) to secure permission directly from Lhasa. After the Tibetan government was assured that this was a genuine and potentially beneficial U.S. government mission, the Tibetan foreign affairs bureau extended the two OSS officers an invitation. They entered Tibet from India carrying presents and a letter from President Franklin Roosevelt to the young fourteenth Dalai Lama asking him to assist the officers. Dated July 3, 1942, the letter said:

> Your HOLINESS: Two of my fellow countrymen, Ilyia Tolstoy and Brooke Dolan, hope to visit your Pontificate and the historic and widely famed city of Lhasa. There are in the United States of America many persons, among them myself, who, long and greatly interested in your land and people, would highly value such an opportunity.
>
> As you know, the people of the United States, in association with those of twenty-seven other countries, are now engaged in a war which has been thrust upon the world by nations bent on conquest who are intent on destroying freedom of thought, of religion, and of action everywhere. The united Nations are fighting today in defense of and for preservation of freedom, confident that we shall be victorious because our cause is just, our capacity is adequate, and our determination is unshakable.
>
> I am asking Ilyia Tolstoy and Brooke Dolan to convey to you a little gift in token of my friendly sentiment toward you.
>
>   With cordial greetings [etc.]
>   Franklin D. Roosevelt[1]

Although this must have looked like government-to-government relations to officials in Lhasa, in Washington it was not considered such. Despite the strong Wilsonian commitment to self-determination in the United States[2] and the 1941 Atlantic Charter in which Roosevelt and Churchill agreed to "respect the right of all people to choose the form of government under which they will live,"[3] the United States refused to support Tibetan independence or its right to self-determination. In this case, Secretary of State Cordell Hull informed President Roosevelt that this letter was addressed to the Dalai Lama in his religious capacity, "rather than in his capacity of secular leader of Tibet, so as not to offend the Chinese Government which includes Tibet in the territory of the Republic of China."[4] This policy made sense given China's importance as a U.S. ally in World War II, but neither the Tibetan government nor the Dalai Lama was informed of this subtlety. Tibetans, therefore, had no reason to assume the letter was not sent to the Dalai Lama as head of Tibet, or that it failed to demonstrate tacit U.S. recognition of Tibet's independence.

A more blatant incident occurred in 1948 when the Tibetan government sent a trade mission to the United States and Britain, using its own passports. British officials in Hong Kong stamped these with entry visas valid for three months. The British visas expired while the Tibetans were in the United States, and when the Tibetans went for what they thought were routine new visas, their request was denied. The Chinese government in the interim had confronted the British government about the potential implications of accepting Tibetan passports when according to its official position it did not accept that Tibet was independent. The British foreign office then reversed itself and assured the Chinese that a mistake had been made, promising that in the future they would issue no more visas on Tibetan passports. The Tibetans were advised to accept entry visas on a separate piece of paper called an "Affidavit of Identity." Surprised and indignant, the delegation refused, saying they would rather not visit Britain than accept this. Since this would have dismayed the friends of Tibet in England, London devised an ingenious solution that truly typifies the double standards rampant at this time. They carefully crossed out the words "three months" on the expired visa stamp and neatly wrote in pen above it, "nine months." This allowed them to keep their promise to the Chinese government not to issue the Tibetans *new* visas on their passports since this was still the original visa.

At the same time they were also able to welcome the Tibetans to Britain on their Tibetan government–issued passports.

It is instructive to contrast Tibet's experiences with those of Mongolia. At the fall of the Qing dynasty Mongolia had a political status parallel to that of Tibet, and like Tibet, sought to become independent. Mongolia, however, underwent a Communist revolution and became part of the Soviet bloc. It maintained extremely close relations with the USSR, with thousands of Russians working in Mongolia and large numbers of Mongolians studying in the Soviet Union. Mongolian troops also fought side by side with their Russian allies against the Japanese in a key battle in 1939 at Nomonkhan, where the Japanese northern advance was stopped.[5] However, like Tibet, Mongolian independence was de facto not de jure, and Chiang Kaishek continued to claim it as part of China.

The Russian victory in WWII quickly changed that. Unlike the Western democracies, the USSR supported Mongolia's claim to independence after World War II. Stalin considered a friendly buffer state important and persuaded President Roosevelt at Yalta to agree to a plebiscite for independence in Mongolia. When the results of the plebiscite unanimously favored independence from China, the USSR and the United States persuaded Chiang Kaishek to accept the vote. As a result, Mongolia today is an independent country and a member of the United Nations.

In contrast, Tibet's political subordination to China was repeatedly validated by the West throughout the first half of the twentieth century, and particularly in the critical years during and immediately following World War II. Despite lofty rhetoric about freedom and self-determination, Western democracies maintained a consistent policy of yielding to Chinese sensibilities, accepting the official Chinese position that Tibet was one of the territories comprised by the Chinese nation.

THE SEVENTEEN-POINT AGREEMENT

The establishment of the PRC in October 1949 set in motion events that two years later broke the deadlock over the Tibet Question.

In its formative years, the Chinese Communist party had followed the Soviet Union's lead and adopted the policy that ethnic territories in China would be autonomous republics with the right of secession. By the end of World War II, however, this policy shifted to political centralism, and when the new Communist government began, its nationality policy held that Communist China would be an indivisibly multiethnic state with autonomous nationality regions (rather than republics) that had no right to secede. Tibet was considered one such nationality region, and in late 1949 the new Chinese Communist government proclaimed its liberation as one of the main goals for the People's Liberation Army (PLA).[6]

The Tibetan government found itself in a very difficult situation. The string of fortuitous events that had prevented China from actively addressing the Tibet Question after the fall of the Qing dynasty were no longer present, so the modernization faction's fear that Tibet would some day have to defend its independence militarily was about to come to pass. Not surprisingly, Tibet's poorly armed and led military had only an amateurish plan to combat an invasion. Moreover, Tibet was more isolated internationally than at any time since 1913 because Britain no longer had any national interest in maintaining Tibet's "autonomous" status. Once it granted independence to India in 1947, London saw its role as supporting India's foreign policy, which at this time centered on establishing friendly relations with the PRC, not Tibet.

Nevertheless, the Tibetan government did not sit by idly. It responded to the Communists' victory in the Chinese civil war by sending appeals to the United States and Great Britain, requesting civil and military assistance in the face of what it perceived as the Communist threat to its independence. The letter to Britain said:

> The Chinese Communist troops have invaded the Chinese Provinces of Lanchow, Chinghai and Sinkiang; and as these Provinces are situated on the border of Tibet, we have sent an official letter to Mr. Mautsetung, leader of the Chinese Communist Government, asking him to respect the territorial integrity of Tibet.
>
> We enclose herewith the true copy of the letter which our Government has sent to the leader of Chinese Communist Government, thinking that he may duly consider the matter. But in case the Chinese communist leader ignores our letter, and takes an aggressive attitude and sends his troops toward Tibet, then the Government of Tibet will be obligated to defend her own country by all possible means. Therefore the Government of Tibet would earnestly desire to request every possible help from your Government.
>
> We would be most grateful if you would please consider extensive aid in respect of requirements for Civil and military purposes, and kindly let us have a favourable reply at your earliest opportunity.
>
> From,
> The Tibetan Foreign Bureau,
> Lhasa [4 November 1949][7]

The Americans were sent a similar appeal. Neither Britain nor America, however, had any interest in encouraging the Tibetans. The United States told the British "they were going to send a reply that would discourage Tibetans from expecting any aid."[8] The receipt of these noncommittal replies from the Western democracies, the main enemy of Communism, was extremely disappointing. But with its options limited, the Tibetan government decided to send missions to the United States and Great Britain (as well as China and Nepal) in the hope that face-to-face contact would generate support. On December 22, 1949, the Tibetan foreign bureau sent the following letter to President Truman and Secretary of State Dean Acheson:

Though Tibet has remained an Independent Country for about thirty years without any trouble, but recently the Chinese Communist leaders have announced over their Radio claiming Tibet as a part of Chinese territory and many other remarks about Tibet which are absolutely baseless and misleading. Besides the Chinese Communists have already occupied the border Provinces of Sinkiang, Sining (the Capital of Chinghai), and also Shikang.[9]

Therefore it is impossible for us to remain indifferent at such a critical time. Hence we are deputing soon Lachag Khenchung Thupten Sanghe and Rimshi Dingja to lead a special Mission to your country for the purpose of obtaining aid from your government.

We would therefore be most grateful to your honour if you would kindly render every possible assistance to our Mission on their arrival in Washington.[10]

The new Communist government protested loudly on learning of this plan, but its concerns were misplaced since the Western democracies were not interested in encouraging Tibetans, in part because they believed that this would make a Chinese invasion of Tibet more likely. They therefore refused to accept the proposed missions. The U.S. government feared that even answering the Tibetans in writing might "be considered by the Tibetans as recognition of their independent status," so the U.S. Embassy in New Delhi was instructed to pass on a verbal reply dissuading the Tibetans from sending the mission.[11] Britain did likewise.

Meanwhile, in China, the government's announcement that a major goal for 1950 was the liberation of Tibet, was not empty talk—Mao Zedong had actually begun planning the strategy for "liberating" Tibet. Mao had an excellent sense of history and understood clearly that Tibet had an international status that set it apart from every other nationality group in China. On one occasion Mao told his generals they had to be patient and go slow in Tibet: "Tibet and Xinjiang are different," he said. "In Xinjiang in the old society there were 200,000–300,000 Chinese but in Tibet there was not even a single Chinese. So our troops are in a place where there were no Chinese in the past."[12] But not only were no Chinese living there, Tibet, as we have seen, dealt with foreign nations directly, signing international agreements of sorts and regulating entry to its territory. And even though Mao had millions of troops under arms, it was not impossible that a determined, well-equipped guerrilla army in the high, frigid mountains of Tibet could create military problems for the People's Liberation Army (PLA). Liberating Tibet militarily could therefore have serious international ramifications and could even draw in the enemies of Communist China such as the United States. Consequently, Mao Zedong believed that China's best strategy was to "liberate" Tibet peacefully; that is, with the agreement of the government of Tibet. This outcome would eliminate the possibility of a lengthy guerrilla war in the mountains of Tibet and reduce the potential for international intervention.

The problem with this strategy was that the Tibetan government was unlikely to renounce its de facto independence voluntarily to become part of Mao's Communist state. Mao therefore believed that military action would likely be needed to force Tibet to the negotiating table (as the British had done in 1903–1904), but he was clear that the goal should be to secure peaceful liberation by agreement. Consequently, in December 1949 Mao ordered preparations for an invasion of political Tibet's eastern province (centered at Chamdo), and by early 1950, the Southwest Military and Civil Bureau[13] in Chongqing was designated to lead the attack. If the Tibetan government did not quickly agree to peaceful liberation, Mao wanted the attack to start as early as the summer of 1950 because he feared that a postponement would give the Tibetans more time to muster international support.

The Chinese Communists tried to persuade the Tibetan government to begin negotiations for "peaceful liberation" by having well-known religious leaders from ethnographic Tibet (Chinese-controlled Qinghai and Sichuan/Xikang provinces) give assurances about religious freedom and so forth. When the Tibetan government vacillated and missed a Chinese-issued deadline for sending a negotiating delegation to Beijing, Mao ordered the PLA's eighteenth army to attack Chamdo. On October 7, 1950, the PLA troops crossed the Yangtse River frontier and attacked the Tibetan troops defending the border. The military goal was not to push through to Lhasa, but rather to cut off and disable the entire ten-thousand-person Tibetan Chamdo army so that it did not retreat further west and set up a new defensive line.

The Tibetan forces were ineptly led and organized. Appointment as a general in the Tibetan army was simply another work rotation for government officials that required no special training, and the soldiers, many of whom were serving as a corvee tax, regularly brought their families with them to the front. Tibet was also employing a flawed defense strategy that the British had told them was hopeless thirteen years earlier. Consequently, when the PLA attacked, it confronted Tibetan troops strung out in small units all along the Yangtse river. Some PLA units quickly broke though the set defense line, encircling and outflanking the Tibetans, and within two weeks the PLA had captured the Tibetan army, including the governor general. The road to the capital was now open as there were virtually no reserve troops between Chamdo and Lhasa. However, in accordance with Mao's Tibet strategy, the PLA stopped its advance and again called for Lhasa to commence negotiations. Mao did not want simply to conquer Tibet, even though it would have been easy to do so. He wanted a political settlement approved by Tibet's leader, the Dalai Lama. He wanted China's claim to Tibet legitimized by having the Dalai Lama accept Chinese sovereignty and work with the PRC gradually to reform Tibet's feudal economy.

The Tibetan government's worst fear was now realized—it was under a military attack that it had no obvious means to counter. Its army did not even have a plan to shift to a guerrilla mode to harass the PLA. Consequently, Tibet again turned for help to the world community, sending appeals to the UN, the United States, India, and Britain. The Tibetan appeal to the UN led to new examinations of the Tibet Question, in particular, whether Tibet was qualified to bring an issue before the UN since it was not a member. Article 35 (section 2) of the UN Charter said that "a state which is not a member may bring to the attention of the Security Council or the General Assembly any dispute to which it is a party if it accepts in advance, for the purposes of the dispute, the obligations of pacific settlement provided in the present Charter."[14] But was Tibet a "state"? The British foreign office examined the issue and concluded that it could qualify as a state,[15] and so could bring an issue before the UN, but as indicated above, the British foreign office also felt that India had the primary responsibility for issues dealing with Tibet, and that Britain should follow the lead of the government of India. London also believed that the UN could not enforce a demand that China withdraw its forces from Tibet and that such a failure would weaken the UN's stature. India, therefore, had a critical role, and unfortunately for Tibet, it was determined not to let Tibet hamper its development of close and friendly relations with China, so was opposed to a UN discussion.[16] Consequently, when the question was raised in the UN by El Salvador, the British and Indian representatives were the first speakers and both recommended that the Tibet issue should not be considered. Thus the proposal was adjourned.

The Tibetan government, disheartened and isolated, concluded that it had no choice but to send a negotiating delegation to Beijing, and did so in the spring of 1951. Much as they had been forced to do in 1904 after the British invasion of Lhasa, these delegates reluctantly signed an agreement on May 23, 1951. It was called the "Seventeen-Point Agreement for the Peaceful Liberation of Tibet."[17]

The Seventeen-Point Agreement ushered in a new chapter in Sino-Tibetan relations since it officially ended the conflict over the Tibet Question. Point 1 sets this out clearly: "The Tibetan people shall unite and drive out imperialist forces from Tibet: the Tibet people shall return to the big family of the Motherland—the People's Republic of China."[18] Tibet, for the first time in its 1,300 years of recorded history, had now in a formal written agreement acknowledged Chinese sovereignty. In exchange for this concession, China, in points 3, 4, 7, and 11, agreed to maintain the Dalai Lama and the traditional political-economic system intact until such time as the Tibetans wanted reforms.

Point 3.   In accordance with the policy towards nationalities laid down in the Common Programme of the Chinese People's Consultative Conference, the Tibetan people have the right of exercising national regional autonomy under the leadership of the Central People's Government.

Point 4.   The central authorities will not alter the existing political system in Tibet. The central authorities also will not alter the established status, functions and powers of the Dalai Lama. Officials of various ranks shall hold office as usual.

Point 7.   . . . The religious beliefs, customs, and habits of the Tibetan People shall be respected, and lama monasteries shall be protected. The Central Authorities will not effect a change in the income of the monasteries.

Point 11.   In matters related to various reforms in Tibet, there will be no compulsion on the part of the central authorities. The local government of Tibet should carry out reforms of its own accord, and when the people raise demands for reform, they shall be settled by means of consultation with the leading personnel of Tibet.[19]

The Seventeen-Point Agreement gave Mao the political settlement he felt was critical to legitimize unambiguously Tibet's status as a part of China. However, this legitimization was achieved by allowing Tibet to retain its feudal-theocratic government and economy, at least for the foreseeable future. Such a concession clearly set Tibet apart from other nationality areas since it was only with Tibet that Beijing entered into a written agreement with the traditional government allowing it to continue to rule.

The Dalai Lama first heard of the signing while he was living at Yadong, the small Tibetan town near the Indian/Sikkim border where he and his top officials had moved in late 1950 preparatory to making a quick escape to India should the Chinese invade Lhasa. The announcement of the signing shocked them since the terms had not been cleared before signing. The Tibetan negotiating team had decided that referring each item to Yadong for discussion would produce endless debate and no agreement would be possible. This would result, they felt, in an all-out Chinese invasion of Tibet that would inevitably end in Tibet's defeat with much loss of life and property and the end of Tibet's Buddhist institutions. Consequently, they agreed to take responsibility for making the best deal they could, knowing that the Dalai Lama could always refuse to accept it.[20]

A heated debate ensued in Yadong regarding how to respond to the agreement. One faction advocated denouncing the agreement and fleeing into exile, while another argued that the Dalai Lama should return to Lhasa and abide by the terms of the accord. The proreturn faction looked to parts of the agreement such as point 4, previously mentioned. The rejection faction, led by lay officials such as Council Minister Surkhang, believed the Chinese could not be trusted to abide by these terms once they controlled the country. They viewed with apprehension the vagueness of point 11, which stated reforms could be made if the Tibetan people wanted them, and point 15, which said that the central government would set up military headquarters and a military and administrative committee in Tibet to ensure the implementation of this agreement. They also disliked the fact that the agreement gave China the right to station troops in Tibet and handle Tibet's defense and foreign affairs. Ultimately they feared that admitting Chinese sovereignty would preclude future claims to independence should the situation change.

The U.S. government and CIA had played a relatively minor role in the Sino-Tibetan conflict up to then, but this was the heyday of the Cold War and the U.S. government's China policy was to harass and obstruct the new Communist state whenever possible. Chinese aggression in Tibet provided a new opportunity to do this, and Washington jumped at the opportunity. However, from the U.S. perspective, charges of Chinese Communist aggression would have little resonance if the Dalai Lama returned to Lhasa and ratified the agreement, so a major effort was made to persuade him to denounce the Seventeen-Point Agreement and flee into exile.

A rash of covert contacts occurred between Tibetan and American officials in India, as well as with the Dalai Lama in Yadong. The United States offered, among other things, to permit the Dalai Lama and a few hundred of his leading officials to move to the United States if he denounced the agreement and left Tibet,[21] but the U.S. declarations of support rang hollow, even to Tibetans inexperienced in modern diplomacy. Despite rhetoric that sang the praises of freedom and self-determination, Washington was not only unwilling to support Tibet as a nation independent of China, but was also unwilling to provide substantial military aid so that Tibetans could effectively launch a guerrilla war against the Chinese in Tibet. The United States would commit only to supporting autonomy for Tibet and to providing "light arms through India."[22] Consequently, the Dalai Lama did not denounce the agreement and flee to India.

It was difficult for Westerners to comprehend how the Dalai Lama could choose to return to a Tibet ruled by Mao, so when some Western "experts" in India suggested that the Dalai Lama was being prevented from fleeing by his own officials in Yadong, the United States concocted a bizarre plan to "free" him, sending the Dalai Lama (on July 17, 1951) a note listing three options for escape:

a. Choose small group of faithful followers and leave [Yadong] quietly with them. This wld presumably involve leaving at night in effort to avoid deputations which have come to Yatung from principal monasteries and from govt at Lhasa to persuade Dalai Lama to return to Lhasa.

b. Order [name excised from file] bring him surreptitiously to India.
    [section of memo excised from file]

c. If neither (a) nor (b) feasible, Dalai Lama to send msg to [name excised from file] requesting [name excised from file] send [Heinrich] Harrer [an Austrian mountaineer who had lived in Lhasa for the past seven years] and [George] Patterson [a British missionary who had lived in eastern Tibet prior to the Communist takeover] secretly and in disguise to meet Dalai Lama near Yatung in accordance with prearranged plan and bring Dalai lama back. Detailed plan for this operation also being conveyed by [name excised from file] but he is to make it clear to Dalai Lama it is to be adopted only as a last resort.[23]

But the whole premise of this operation was absurd. The Dalai Lama was in Yadong not as a "captive" but because he and the majority of his officials found the U.S. offer lacking. From their point of view, the United States was unwilling to commit to what they sought—active and energetic U.S. diplomatic and military assistance to establish Tibet as an independent country recognized by the United Nations. The United States was willing to send its troops to Korea, but not even to recognize Tibet was an independent country, let alone arm and train Tibetans to launch a guerrilla war in Tibet. By contrast, if the Dalai Lama accepted the agreement and returned to Lhasa, the old political system would remain intact with himself at its head. And there was hope that he could gradually persuade the Chinese to allow the core of Tibetan culture and religion to continue.

Ironically, the young Dalai Lama was not at all opposed to the idea of social reforms, nor was he wedded to the need to maintain the exploitive traditional feudal system in Tibet. In an interview in 1994 he recalled:

> I myself from small liked the idea of mechanical schools. I thought we should have schools, and machines from when I was small.
>
> The road from Phari to Lhasa was there from the British period, but even though it wasn't a car road I thought at the time it would be easy to make it into one . . . and I strongly felt that it would be good to have a vehicle road.
>
> When we arrived in Gyantse [town] I had heard that the Phala family had a small school there, and I had strong feelings about improving schools in the rural areas, and we talked about that. I also thought that taxes like the corvee labor taxes, were extremely bad, and I also did not like the difficult custom [of people being saddled with] old debts [passed down from generation to generation]. When I was small the sweepers [in the palace] told me about these things.[24]

Consequently, the possibility that the Dalai Lama and China could reach an accommodation on change and modernization was plausible, and the Dalai Lama accepted the opinion of the majority of lay and monastic leaders, returning to Lhasa in August 1951. Chinese troops moved peacefully into Lhasa in the fall of 1951.

The Seventeen-Point Agreement established a written set of mutually agreed-upon ground rules for Tibetan-Chinese interaction and held out the promise that Tibet could function as part of the People's Republic of China without losing its distinctive way of life. This was far less than the autonomy discussed at Simla, but it was a formula China officially accepted. The Dalai

Lama indicated his formal acceptance of it through a telegram sent to Mao Zedong in late October 1951. Both sides, however, soon found that operationalizing the terms of the Seventeen-Point Agreement was neither straightforward nor easy.

COEXISTENCE UNDER THE
SEVENTEEN-POINT AGREEMENT

In the years immediately following the signing of the Seventeen-Point Agreement, Mao Zedong, contrary to popular belief in the West, pursued a policy of moderation in Tibet. Although his ultimate aim was clearly to transform Tibet in accordance with socialist goals, his Tibet strategy sought to create cordial relations between Han (ethnic Chinese) and Tibetans, and allay Tibetan anxieties so that Tibet's elite would over time genuinely accept "reintegration" with China and agree to a societal transformation. Calling themselves "New Chinese," the PLA troops and officials in Tibet emphasized that they had come to help improve conditions in Tibet, not exploit and abuse it, and took care to show respect for Tibetan culture and religion. For example, they gave alms to all twenty thousand of the monks in the Lhasa area. This rhetoric was supported by a strict behavioral code that precluded the PLA from taking anything against the will of the people, and required them to pay for goods and services in old Chinese silver coins (rather than paper money). The policy also allowed the old feudal and monastic systems to continue unchanged. Between 1951 and 1959, not only was no aristocratic or monastic property confiscated, but feudal lords were permitted to exercise continued judicial authority over their hereditarily bound peasants. At the heart of this strategy was the Dalai Lama. Mao saw him, in particular, as the vehicle by which the feudal and religious elites (and then the masses) would come to accept their place in China's new multiethnic Communist state. Mao's Tibet policy in this period was therefore one of gradualism. Military and administrative infrastructures should be developed, but Chinese officials in Tibet should not prematurely try to force change.[25]

Mao's policy, however, encountered many problems. Within the Communist party, one clique led by Fan Ming argued that the party should back Tibet's second greatest incarnation, the Panchen Lama, since he was politically a "progressive." And despite Mao's views about the need for a policy of gradualism, many of the PLA's battle-hardened commanders in Tibet found it difficult to show respect for the feudal elites and sit by and leave the old system intact. Chinese officials in Tibet actually made plans to begin political and economic reforms in 1956, although they were never implemented due to intervention by Mao Zedong.

However, the situation in ethnographic Tibet was very different since these Tibetans were not part of political Tibet (or the Seventeen-Point Agreement). Therefore, when Sichuan province became caught up in the nationwide "socialist transformation of agriculture" campaign in 1955–1956, so did these areas. In late 1955 Li Jingquan, the party secretary in Sichuan, authorized the start of democratic reforms throughout his province, including minority areas. This quickly led to a bloody rebellion in Tibetan areas, which spilled over into political Tibet as refugees (and rebels) from ethnographic Tibet fled to the safety of Lhasa and its environs. They became a major factor precipitating the 1959 uprising in Lhasa.

Among Tibetans in political Tibet, Mao's policy also encountered serious problems. Although a small faction in the Tibetan government led by Council Minister Ngabö advocated that Tibetans themselves should quickly reform their feudal institutions, this perspective had no broad support. Ngabö's analogy that the hat one makes oneself will fit far better than one made by someone else fell on deaf ears. And while the Dalai Lama liked and respected Ngabö and was in favor of trying to reach an operational compromise with the Chinese (including some modern reforms for Tibet),[26] he was unable (or unwilling) to control anti-Chinese activists in his government. From the beginning, therefore, ultranationalistic, hard-line Tibetans created a confrontational and adversarial atmosphere. As in the 1920s, the conservative Tibetan faction simply did not want change. They felt Tibet was unique and perfect as it was. Moreover, they felt that because Tibet had been forced into the agreement with China through the invasion of Chamdo, they were not really bound by its terms. Consequently, rather than try to reach an accommodation with the Chinese, they created unpleasant conditions in Lhasa, especially food shortages, as leverage to persuade the Chinese to withdraw all but a few of their troops and officials. This, of course, was the same basic strategy that Tibetan officials had used in the eighteenth century with the Qing dynasty garrisons.

By the mid-1950s the situation inside Tibet began to deteriorate. Chinese hardliners were pushing to begin "socialist transformation" reforms in Tibet proper, and Tibetan hardliners in league with refugees from the failed uprising in ethnographic Tibet were organizing an armed rebellion. Moreover, the United States was encouraging the anti-Chinese faction and in 1957 actually started to train and arm Tibetan guerrillas. Mao made a last attempt to salvage his gradualist policy in 1957 when he reduced the number of Han cadre and troops in Tibet and promised the Dalai Lama in writing that China would not implement socialist land reforms in political Tibet for the next six years. Furthermore, at the end of that period, Mao stated that he would postpone reforms again if conditions were not ripe.[27] The Dalai Lama, however, could not quell the unrest within Tibet, and in March 1959 an uprising broke out in Lhasa that ended with his flight into exile in India. The Dalai Lama then renounced the Seventeen-Point Agreement and sought support for Tibet's independence and self-determination. The Tibet Question now reemerged as an international issue. Mao's "gradualist" policy had failed.

The Tibetan rebellion also failed dismally. The CIA's support for the guerrillas was too little too late, and the Tibetan guerrilla forces were unable to achieve their initial hope of holding some territory within Tibet as a "Free Tibet" base of operations. The CIA subsequently assisted the guerrillas in establishing a safe-haven base of operations in northern Nepal, but the subsequent raids into Tibet from Nepal had no impact on the political situation in Tibet.

Meanwhile, the Chinese government in Tibet also renounced the Seventeen-Point Agreement and terminated the traditional government. It confiscated the estates of the religious and secular elites, closed down most of Tibet's several thousand monasteries, and created a new Communist governmental structure.[28] Tibet's special status as a theocratic political entity within the Chinese Communist state was now ended.

The 1951–1959 transition period therefore ended poorly for both Tibet and China. Tibet's power elite was unable to develop and implement a realistic strategy that could either induce the Chinese to leave or create a niche within China in which they could maximize long-term autonomy. Different elements in the Tibetan elite pursued contradictory policies, resulting in a premature and ineffective military confrontation that led to the destruction of the old society, including Buddhist monasticism and all that they were seeking to preserve. On the Chinese side, ideological zeal in prematurely implementing socialist changes thwarted any chance of winning over Tibetans to being part of socialist China.

However, some in China saw the failure as the result of Mao's flawed moderation policy. Throughout the 1950s there were grumblings within the Chinese Communist party about this policy, particularly what some considered Mao's misguided views about the Dalai Lama, who they felt was duplicitous, giving the impression he was in favor of change when he was really pursuing "splittist" policies—that is, trying to split Tibet out from under Chinese control. These elements quietly blamed this policy for the 1959 rebellion and the reinternation-alization of the Tibet Question, and today some in China consider it one of the party's (Mao's) greatest failures.[29]

After 1959, both the Tibetan exiles and China competed to legitimize their own representations of Tibetan history and current events. The Chinese talked about the extreme cruelty and abuses of the old feudal system and serfdom, and the Tibetans in exile talked about a host of Chinese cultural and human rights violations, including genocide. This confrontation of "representations" continues to the present.

The Tibetan exiles initially fared well in this representational competition. The Tibet issue was raised in the UN with the help of the United States—the CIA actually funding the exile Tibetan's law firm. The UN resolutions on Tibet (passed in 1961 and 1965) used language that supported Tibet's claim to self-determination:

> [The General Assembly is] *Gravely concerned* at the continuation of events in Tibet, including the violation of the fundamental human rights of the Tibetan people and the suppression of the distinctive cultural and religious life which they have traditionally enjoyed,
>
> *Noting with deep anxiety* the severe hardships which these events have inflicted on the Tibetan people, as evidenced by the large-scale exodus of Tibetan refugees to the neighboring countries,
>
> *Considering* that these events violate fundamental human rights and freedoms set out in the Charter of the United Nations and the Universal Declaration of Human Rights, including the principle of self-determination of peoples and nations, and have the deplorable effect of increasing international tension and embittering relations between peoples,
>
> 1. *Reaffirms* its conviction that respect for the principles of the Charter of the United Nations and the Universal Declaration of Human Rights is essential for the evolution of a peaceful world order based on the rule of law;
> 2. *Solemnly renews* its call for the cessation of practices which deprive the Tibetan people of their fundamental human

rights and freedoms, including their right to self-determination;

3. *Expresses the hope* that Member States will make all possible efforts, as appropriate, towards achieving the purposes of the present solution.[30]

A report by the International Commission of Jurists in 1959 also stated that Tibet was "to all intents and purposes an independent country and had enjoyed a large degree of sovereignty."[31]

Moreover, the United States moved a bit beyond its previous position of recognizing Tibet only as an autonomous country under the suzerainty of China by mentioning the right of Tibetans to self-determination. The 1960 response of Secretary of State Christian E. Herter to a letter from the Dalai Lama illustrates the new language: "As you know, while it has been the historical position of the US to consider Tibet as an autonomous *country* under the suzerainty of China, the American people have also traditionally stood for the principle of self-determination. It is the belief of the US government that this principle should apply to the people of Tibet and that they *should have the determining voice in their own political destiny*" (emphasis added).[32]

However, the Dalai Lama and his representatives had been seeking UN and U.S. support of Tibet's independent status, and this the United States was unwilling to provide. The U.S. argument in the following document [dated October 14, 1959] reveals a continuing refusal to recognize Tibetan independence despite deep involvement in training and funding a large Tibetan guerrilla operation at the time:

> FE [Far Eastern Affairs] has completed a study . . . of the question of the United States recognition of the independence of Tibet in which the considerations both for and against such action are examined in detail. Taking these factors into account, we have concluded that on balance the arguments against recognition of Tibetan independence under present conditions

are stronger than those in favor. I consider this conclusion valid from the standpoint of both United States national interest and from that of the Tibetans. We share with the Tibetans the objective of keeping the Tibetans' cause alive in the consciousness of the world and maintaining the Dalai Lama as an effective spokesman of the Tibetan people. I believe that United States recognition of the Dalai Lama's government as that of an independent country would serve neither purpose well. Since very few countries could be expected to follow our lead, our recognition now would make the Dalai Lama the leader of a government-in-exile obviously dependent on the United States for political support. This would almost certainly damage the prestige and influence he now enjoys as one of Asia's revered leaders and would hamper his activities on behalf of the Tibetan people.

Nonetheless, there remains the need for the United States to appear responsive to the Dalai Lama's appeal and take a stand conforming to our historic position as a supporter of the principle of the self-determination of peoples.[33]

Consequently, for the exiles,[34] the hope that the United States would exert leadership in garnering world support for their independence was flawed from the beginning, and certainly ended in the late 1960s when President Nixon and National Security Advisor Kissinger moved to establish rapprochement with China. At this point, the United States withdrew its backing for the Nepal-based Tibetan guerrillas and the operation collapsed within a few years. Moreover, beginning in about 1966, the official U.S. position ceased talking about "self-determination" for Tibet, or even of Tibet as an autonomous country as it had in Herter's statement in 1960.

With policy focused on improving its accommodation with China, Tibet became an embarrassment for the United States. Not only was the Tibet Question no longer relevant to U.S. national interests—in fact, it was potentially harmful. By the 1970s, therefore, shifting world alignments placed the Tibetan exiles in a much weakened position.

Consequently, the exiles' post-1959 efforts had no impact on the situation in Tibet and did nothing to create an international consensus over its right to self-determination or independence. The Chinese Communist Party restructured Tibet's farming and nomadic pastoral areas into communes, and, under the banner of the Cultural Revolution and the "Four Olds" campaign, placed Tibetan traditional culture and religion under severe attack. Between the rebellions, food shortages, and struggle sessions against "class enemies," Tibet suffered substantial privation. The full loss of life is still not clearly known, but the damage to Tibet's culture was substantial.

A Tibetan who returned to China in 1964 after attending college in the United States poignantly recalled in his autobiography his impressions of Lhasa when he returned with the Red Guards in 1966:

> We stayed in Lhasa for four or five months. . . . A decade had passed since I left Lhasa for India, and a great deal had changed. As I initially looked around, I was struck by the many new houses, building and roads. . . . I was particularly impressed with the many trees lining the highways. . . . However, I quickly learned that physical changes weren't the whole story. . . .
>
> One of the biggest changes in the city itself was the absence of a lively central market. There was nothing on sale on the streets anymore. Gone were the cramped booths heaped full of wares, the voices of salesmen and customers laughing and haggling, and the many tea and beer shops I used to frequent. In their place were a few poorly stocked government stores.
>
> It also soon became clear that the people weren't very well fed, either. Food was rationed, and there was almost no meat or butter or potatoes. I had lived in the old Lhasa for many years and was under no illusions about its shortcomings. However, there had always been a lot of food, and if you had any money to spend at all you had quite a bit of freedom and choice. Now the food was rationed at low levels. . . .
>
> Perhaps the most striking difference I saw was that the people in general seemed dispirited and sullen. They appeared forlorn, as if they had just lost a close friend or relative.[35]

Another recollection illustrates the magnitude of religious persecution:

> I also met a woman . . . who would . . . later become my wife. . . .
> By all rights, Sangyela was in no danger of being struggled
> against because she was definitely from the proletarian class, but
> she was also extremely religious and hated the government for
> closing the monasteries and prohibiting all religion, even in your
> own home. If a neighbor or cadre [official] found out you were
> still practicing religion and reported you, you would be brought
> before the masses and struggled against, for the goal of the
> Cultural Revolution was to eradicate all remnants of old values,
> customs, and beliefs. But we Tibetans are a stubborn people, and
> many Tibetans from all classes and backgrounds risked punish-
> ment and struggle sessions by secretly saying prayers in their
> homes or by circumambulating holy temples as if they were just
> on a stroll, all the while whispering silent prayers. Sangyela was
> one of these. In her case, she went so far as to continue to burn
> butter lamps as offerings to the gods. She would save small am-
> mounts of butter from her scanty monthly ration and use it to
> light a small butter lamp which she placed inside the cabinet that
> used to be her altar (behind its closed doors) rather than on top, as
> was normally done. When she told me this all I could think about
> was the danger of setting the whole house on fire by leaving a
> burning lamp inside the old, dry wooden cabinet.[36]

In brief, therefore, in the period after the 1959 uprising,
Buddhism was destroyed and Tibetans were forced to abandon
deeply held values and customs that went to the core of their
cultural identity. The class struggle sessions and the constant
barrage of propaganda contradicting and ridiculing everything they understood and felt, sought to destroy the social
and cultural fabric of the Tibetans' traditional way of life.
These were terrible times for Tibetans in Tibet.[37]

The Post-Mao Era

The death of Mao Zedong in 1976, the subsequent fall of the "Gang of Four," and the rise to power of Deng Xiaoping produced major changes in China that included a new cultural and economic ideology, normalization of relations with the United States, and new initiatives to reconcile two outstanding conflicts that concerned the unity of the People's Republic of China—Taiwan and the Tibet Question.

China made a number of unilateral gestures in Tibet in 1978, such as releasing a group of prisoners, announcing that Tibetans would be able to visit relatives abroad, and issuing visas to visit Tibet to a group of private Tibetans living in exile. These moves developed quickly into an "external" strategy intended to solve the Tibet Question by persuading the Dalai Lama and his followers to return to China. Informal talks took place in Hong Kong in 1978 between representatives of the Chinese government and the Dalai Lama's elder brother Gyalo Thondup (who lives in Hong Kong and speaks fluent Chinese); both sides expressed an interest in reconciling the Tibetan Question. Soon after, in 1979, Deng Xiaoping invited Gyalo Thondup to Beijing and told him that apart from the question of total independence all other issues could be discussed and all problems could be resolved. He also said that the Dalai Lama could send fact-finding delegations to Tibet in 1979–1980 to observe conditions there.[1] Beijing obviously believed that the delegations would be impressed by the progress that had been made in Tibet since 1959 and by the solidarity of the Tibetan people with the nation. China also felt that after twenty years in exile the Dalai Lama would be eager for rapprochement with the new, more "liberal" leaders of China. The Dalai Lama responded by sending three fact-finding delegations to China, in which members of his family participated.

Ren Rong, the Han first secretary of the Communist party in Tibet, had been reporting to Beijing that political conditions in Tibet were excellent and that Tibetans were solidly behind the party and the motherland. However, when one of these delegations, including another brother of the Dalai Lama, visited Tibetan areas in Qinghai province, it received a tumultuous welcome. Beijing was embarrassed by this expression of support for the Dalai Lama and contacted Ren in Lhasa asking him what would happen if the delegation were to continue to Lhasa according to plan. Ren is said to have replied that the people of Lhasa were more ideologically developed than the simple farmers and herders of Amdo and strongly supported the ideals of the Communist party; there would be no such problems there. So strongly did the local administration in Tibet believe this that the TAR (Tibet Autonomous Region) government organized neighborhood meetings in Lhasa just before the arrival of the delegation to exhort the local Tibetan "masses" not to let their hatred of the "old society" provoke them to throw stones or spit at the Dalai Lama's delegates who were coming as guests of the Chinese government. The Lhasan masses agreed politely and then gave the delegation a welcome surpassing anything it had received in Qinghai. Thousands upon thousands of Lhasans mobbed the delegation. Many cried and prostrated, others offered ceremonial scarves, fighting to touch the Dalai Lama's brother, and a few shouted Tibetan nationalistic slogans such as "Tibet is independent" and "Han go home." Since Beijing officials accompanied the Tibetan refugee delegation, there was no way that Ren, who was known to be unsympathetic to Tibetan cultural, religious, and language reforms, could cover up this fiasco and his utter misreading of the sentiment of the Tibetan masses.

Thus, contrary to what the Chinese had expected, these visits revealed to the exiles that Chinese proclamations of socialist progress in Tibet had little substance. The living standard of the Tibetan people was poor, economic development minimal, and the destruction of religion and monasticism almost total. They also revealed that the Tibetan masses, despite twenty years of Communist propaganda, still believed strongly in the Dalai Lama and had strong feelings of Tibetan nationalism. Twenty years under China apparently had not extinguished Tibetans' belief in the sanctity of the Dalai Lama and his position as leader of the Tibetan people. It also apparently had not extinguished their feeling that Tibet should be ruled by Tibetans in accordance with Tibetan values. If the "liberation" and incorporation of Tibet into China had been aimed at winning the hearts and minds of the common people, Chinese policies and actions from 1959 to 1980 had not succeeded. The overall impact of the delegations was precisely the opposite of what Beijing had hoped: it bolstered the confidence of the exiles at a difficult time in their history.[2]

Beijing's external strategy was paralleled by a new internal strategy that sought to resolve the Tibet Question by improving economic conditions in Tibet in a manner that met the ethnic sensibilities of Tibetans. After considerable preliminary investigation, the Communist party convened a major Tibet Work Conference in Beijing in early 1980. The following statement from that conference illustrates the new attitude: "We have been established [in Tibet] for thirty years. Now the international situation is very complicated. If we do not seize the moment and immediately improve the relationship between the nationalities [Han and Tibetan] we will make a serious mistake. All the members of the Party must recognize the seriousness and we must reach a consensus."[3] Soon after, in May of 1980, Party Secretary Hu Yaobang and Vice-Premier Wan Li made an unprecedented fact-finding visit to Tibet to see conditions for themselves and determine whether the plan of the

Tibet Work Conference needed revision. They were apparently dismayed by what they saw and heard, finding it worse than they had anticipated. Hu publicly announced a liberal six-point reform program for Tibet, which included among its salient points:

(1) Full play must be given to the right of regional autonomy of minority nationalities *under the unified leadership of the party Central Committee....*

The right to decide for oneself under unified leadership should not be abolished. It is necessary fully and independently to exercise this right. Anything that is not suited to Tibet's conditions should be rejected or modified, along with anything that is not beneficial to national unity or the development of production. The autonomous region should fully exercise its right to decide for itself under the unified leadership of the party central committee, and it should lay down laws, rules and regulations according to its special characteristics to protect the right of national autonomy and its special national interests.[4]

(2) ... Compared with other provinces and autonomous regions of the country, it is conspicuous that in Tibet the people's living standards lag far behind. This situation means that the burden of the masses must be considerably lightened. The people in Tibet should be exempt from paying taxes and meeting purchase quotas for the next few years.... All kinds of exactions must be abolished. The people should not be assigned any additional work without pay. Peasants' and herdsmen's produce may be purchased at negotiated prices or bartered to supply mutual needs, and they should be exempt from meeting state purchase quotas....

(3) Specific and flexible policies suited to conditions in Tibet must be carried out on the whole economic front of the region, including the agricultural, animal husbandry, financial and trade, commercial, handicraft and communication fronts, with a view of promoting Tibet's economic development more rapidly......

(5) *So long as the socialist orientation is upheld, vigorous efforts must be made to revive and develop Tibetan culture, education and science.* The Tibetan people have a long history and a

rich culture. The world renowned ancient Tibetan culture included fine Buddhism, graceful music and dance as well as medicine and opera, all of which are worthy of serious study and development. All ideas that ignore and weaken Tibetan culture are wrong. It is necessary to do a good job in inheriting and developing Tibetan culture.

Education has not progressed well in Tibet. Taking Tibet's special characteristics into consideration, efforts should be made to set up universities and middle and primary schools in the region. Some cultural relics and Buddhist scriptures in temples have been damaged, and conscientious effort should be made to protect, sort and study them. Cadres of Han nationality working in Tibet should learn the spoken and written Tibetan language. It should be a required subject; otherwise they will be divorced from the masses. Cherishing the people of minority nationalities is not empty talk. The Tibetan people's habits, customs, history and culture must be respected.

(6) The party's policy on minority cadre must be correctly implemented and the unity between Han and Tibetan cadres must be even more closely enhanced. . . . Full time cadres of Tibetan nationality should account for more than 2/3rds of all government functionaries in Xizang [Tibet], within the next 2–3 years [emphasis added].[5]

This rather remarkable public statement is said to be mild compared to the secret report and speeches Hu Yaobang made to the party cadre, one part of which is said to have equated the previous twenty years of Chinese development efforts in Tibet with throwing money into the Lhasa River.

This decision of Hu Yaobang and the Central Committee of the CCP represents a retreat from the hard-line assimilation policy of the Cultural Revolution and a return to Mao's more ethnically sensitive strategy of the 1950s. The new policy had two main components: (1) an ethnic dimension—making the Tibet Autonomous Region more Tibetan in overall character by fostering a revitalization of Tibetan culture and religion, including more extensive use of Tibetan language, and by withdrawing large numbers of Chinese cadre and replacing them with Tibetans; and (2) an economic dimension—rapidly improving the standard of living of individual Tibetans by temporarily eliminating taxes and "below-market" quota sales, and developing infrastructure to allow Tibet to grow economically in the years ahead.

However, Beijing was no longer willing to permit a separate, non-Communist Tibetan government in Lhasa, as it had in the 1950s—Tibet would continue to be ruled by the CCP.[6] This is the "unified leadership" to which Hu Yaobang referred. While Tibetan culture, language, and ethnicity would be enhanced, and Han Chinese working in Tibet would have to learn Tibetan, Tibetans could control their region only through Tibetan Communist cadres under the auspices of the CCP. Despite Deng Xiaoping's comment that all issues other than independence could be discussed, Communist control was, in fact, simply a given. Rapprochement from the Chinese perspective meant the Dalai Lama had to return to a Tibet ruled by the Chinese Communist party.

Nevertheless, this new policy represented Beijing's attempt to redress the wrongs that had been done to Tibetans and in the process win their trust and support, albeit within the framework that Tibet was an inalienable part of China. These changes were meant to answer critics outside Tibet while at the same time demonstrating to Tibetans in Tibet that being a part of China was in their interests. Nor was this all just propaganda. Although many of the Han and Tibetan officials in Tibet strongly disagreed with this new policy, China implemented various aspects of Hu's general program in the period immediately after 1980. Individual religious practices reappeared on a massive scale throughout Tibet, monasteries reopened (with certain restrictions), and new child monks poured in to resurrect the old tradition. Signs in Tibetan were mandated on shops and official buildings, offices serving the public were instructed to use the Tibetan language in their dealings with citizens, the number of Tibetan officials was increased, plans were made to improve education in Tibetan language, and a number of Chinese cadre left.[7] And not only were exile Tibetans welcome to return for visits, but resident Tibetans could also travel abroad to visit their relatives.

As this internal strategy emerged, Beijing also pursued its external strategy with the Dalai Lama. Informal discussions continued during the 1979–1981 period, including the following letter sent by the Dalai Lama to Deng Xiaoping on March 23, 1981:

> The three fact-finding delegations have been able to find out both the positive and negative aspects of the situation in Tibet. If the Tibetan people's identity is preserved and if they are genuinely happy, there is no reason to complain. However, in reality over 90% of the Tibetans are suffering both mentally and physically, and are living in deep sorrow. These sad conditions had not been brought about by natural disasters, but by human actions. Therefore, genuine efforts must be made to solve the problem in accordance with the existing realities in a reasonable way.
>
> In order to do this, we must improve the relationship *between China and Tibet* as well as between Tibetans in and outside Tibet. With truth and equality as our foundation, we must try to develop friendship between Tibetans and Chinese in the future through better understanding. The time has come to apply our common wisdom in a spirit of tolerance and broad-mindedness to achieve genuine happiness for the Tibetan people with a sense of urgency. On my part, I remain committed to contribute to the welfare of all human beings and in particular the poor and the weak to the best of my ability without making any distinction based on national boundaries. I hope you will let me know your views on the foregoing points (emphasis added).[8]

The tone of this letter was moderate and encouraging given that exiles normally demanded self-determination and independence. However, it also continued to talk of Tibet and China as separate entities. The Chinese government did not respond directly, instead commenting on the Tibet Question when the Dalai Lama's brother Gyalo Thondup secretly met

Hu Yaobang in Beijing on July 28, 1981. At this meeting Hu articulated five points on which rapprochement with the Dalai Lama should be built:

1. The Dalai Lama should be confident that China has entered a new stage of long-term political stability, steady economic growth and mutual help among all nationalities.

2. The Dalai Lama and his representatives should be frank and sincere with the central government, not beat around the bush. There should be no more quibbling over the events in 1959.

3. The central authorities sincerely welcome the Dalai Lama and his followers to come back to live. This is based on the hope that they will contribute to upholding China's unity and promoting solidarity between the Han and Tibetan nationalities, and among all nationalities, and the modernization program.

4. The Dalai Lama will enjoy the same political status and living conditions as he had before 1959. It is suggested that he not go to live in Tibet or hold local posts there. Of course, he may go back to Tibet from time to time. His followers need not worry about their jobs and living conditions. These will only be better than before.

5. When the Dalai Lama wishes to come back, he can issue a brief statement to the press. It is up to him to decide what he would like to say in the statement.[9]

This position, which at the time was not made public, reflected the Chinese government's preferred view that the Tibet Question was fundamentally a dispute between China and the Dalai Lama rather than between the government of China and the Tibetan "government-in-exile." It also conveyed the Chinese unwillingness to consider a compromise in which Tibet would enjoy a different political system from the rest of China. If the Dalai Lama returned, he would "enjoy the same political status and living conditions as he had before 1959," but not live in Tibet or hold positions there, meaning presumably that he would be given a semihonorary position such as vice-chairman of the National People's Congress and would be taken care of financially. The political system in Tibet would therefore continue to be ruled by the Communist party. He and his followers would return as individuals, not as a new government, and they would have to "contribute to upholding China's unity and promoting solidarity between the Han and Tibetan nationalities." Although it was not part of this statement, China's quid pro quo was to permit a distinctly Tibetan ethnic/cultural identity (including Buddhism) in Tibet, and to devote resources to improve the Tibetan standard of living.

Beijing was clearly interested in persuading the Dalai Lama to return to China. From its vantage point, finalizing the right kind of rapprochement would end its problems in Tibet. The return of the Dalai Lama would relegitimize Chinese sovereignty over Tibet, end the international dialogue over the Tibet Question, and persuade the masses of Tibetans genuinely to accept their position within the People's Republic of China. The danger, of course, was that the wrong kind of rapprochement could very well create new pressures for separatism in Tibet, or worse, foment a new uprising. Consequently, it was critical to maintain political control over Tibet. Nevertheless, the Chinese were optimistic because they felt that their willingness to let Tibetan culture, religion, and language flourish, and their commitment to help Tibet develop economically, made this an attractive package. With this in mind, the Dalai Lama was invited to send a negotiating delegation to Beijing.[10] The Dalai Lama accepted, and in October 1982, three exile representatives arrived to begin what might have been a new chapter in Sino-Tibetan relations.

The problem facing the Dalai Lama and his leaders was how to respond to the Chinese at these meetings. The five-point policy outlined by Hu Yaobang had been a great disappointment to the Dalai Lama. Notwithstanding Deng's rhetoric, in essence everything excluding independence was not on the table for real negotiation. Consequently, should he and his officials accept less than total political autonomy, and if so, how much less? Although they strongly felt that history provided convincing evidence of Tibet's independence, at least from the fall of the Qing dynasty in 1911, they also understood that Tibet was now under the physical control of a powerful China, which Tibetans could not defeat on the battlefield. The focal decision, therefore, was whether to adopt a hard-line approach that held out for real political control on the assumption that time was on their side, or to adopt a more conciliatory posture in the belief that genuine political autonomy was unattainable and that this was a unique opportunity to preserve a culturally and ethnically "Tibetan" Tibet. These very difficult choices prompted months of in-depth discussions among the top officials in Dharamsala.

The Chinese five points represented a level of compromise that was very difficult for the Dalai Lama and his leaders to even contemplate. For two decades the Tibetan government-in-exile's rhetoric had adamantly articulated Tibet's right to complete independence and had depicted the Chinese Communists as bestial, untrustworthy oppressors without a shred of humanity or honesty. Suddenly appearing willing to return to live under a Chinese Communist government, therefore, could easily undermine the legitimacy of the Dalai Lama and the exile government among the refugee community. The exile leaders also genuinely worried whether history would depict them as traitors who threw away Tibet's right to independence forever. This was a powerful emotional issue that was hard to intellectualize in an impersonal, cost-benefit, *realpolitik* fashion. One member of the Tibetan negotiating team commented that at first he found it hard to even smile and shake the hands of his Chinese counterparts. The Tibet Question had suddenly become more than a contest of "representations" in the world arena—the Dalai Lama and his officials held the fate of Tibetans in their hands and had to weigh carefully the potential effects on future generations of Tibet.

Complicating this was the future status of "ethnographic Tibet." The exile government was deeply committed to the re-creation of a "Greater" Tibet, which would include in one administrative unit both political and ethnographic Tibet. Such had been the goal of previous Tibetan governments (as at the Simla talks in 1913–1914) and it was deeply cherished, but it was especially important in exile because of the large numbers of Tibetan refugees from those ethnic areas. The Dalai Lama had worked hard since 1959 to meld the disparate refugees into a unified community by including Tibetans from ethnographic Tibet as equals in the exile government, and by setting as a fundamental political objective the inclusion of their areas in a future "free" Tibet. However, the goal of a Greater Tibet was not at all politically realistic. Tibet had not ruled most of these areas for a century or more, and it is difficult to see how China could have handed over large areas in Sichuan, Qinghai, Gansu, and Yunnan, many of which included Chinese and Chinese Muslim (Hui) populations that had migrated there well before the Communists came to power in 1949. However, if Dharamsala decided not to pursue a demand for a Greater Tibet, it would be breaking faith with the Eastern Tibetans in exile. Like the forsaking of independence, this issue was highly contentious and if it became known that the Dalai Lama was willing to consider it, the unity of the exile community could be permanently split.

Working in tandem with these constraints against concilia-tion and compromise was the view of leaders in Dharamsala that they, in a sense, held the upper hand. The visits of their fact-finding delegations had revealed that the majority of the people of Tibet were behind the Dalai Lama, so they felt they brought a powerful chip to the bargaining table—the Tibetan people's loyalty. Consequently, despite the overwhelming power of China and the absence of Western governmental sup-port for Tibetan independence, they felt that China could not solve the Tibet Question without them. In retrospect, this seems somewhat simplistic and naive, but to the Dalai Lama and his top officials in 1982 it was enough to tilt the balance in favor of holding fast and making no compromises. They in effect concluded that time was on their side.

In the end, therefore, there was no consensus in Dharamsala as to political and territorial concessions, and there was pressure *not* to create one for the negotiations in Beijing. Dharamsala consequently sent its high-level representatives to Beijing with a brief to talk only in general terms; for example, to present historical arguments about Tibet and Sino-Tibetan relations. The discussions, therefore, did not get down to substantive issues concerning the terms of the Dalai Lama's return. The Tibetans made only a single comment about their political position, stating *in passing* that if China was willing to offer Taiwan the "one country–two systems" option, Tibet should receive far more.

The Chinese were disappointed by the Tibetans' attitude. They had hoped the exiles would come ready to discuss specifics about their return in a friendly and forthcoming manner, and were frustrated when they persisted in talking about general issues and the "priest-patron relationship" in a way that indicated they were not ready to accept a Tibet that was under the "unified leadership" of the CCP. Like the exile leaders' overassessment of their leverage, this expectation was simplistic and naive. Beijing wanted rapprochement, but did not want to enter into a genuine give-and-take with the exiles over the issue of changes in political control of the Tibet Autonomous Region. In the end, this historic meeting produced no new movement toward solving the Tibet Question, and it raised serious questions in Beijing about the feasibility of rapprochement with the Dalai Lama.

In the aftermath of the 1982 meeting the exile leadership showed some goodwill by refraining from commenting on the meetings, but at the same time continued to attack Chinese policies and human rights violations in Tibet,[11] often going beyond what the actual situation warranted; for example, with charges of Chinese genocide. Dharamsala still felt more comfortable waging the adversarial "representation" battle than adopting a new demeanor that sent clear signals to Beijing that the Dalai Lama was ready to work to develop new friendship and harmony.

On the Chinese side, opponents of Hu Yaobang's Tibet moderation policy interpreted the Dalai Lama's unwillingness to get down to substantive issues and his officials' continuation of attacks as a sign of their insincerity. In fact, some explicitly saw this as déjà vû—a replay of what they considered the duplicitous behavior of the Dalai Lama and his government in the 1950s. Beijing therefore moved to intensify its internal strategy by allocating increased funds for development. This policy was finalized at the Second Tibet Work Conference held in Beijing in 1984. It approved forty-two major construction projects in the Tibet Autonomous Region and extended China's "open door" policy to Tibet, despite the concerns of some leaders and experts that this would draw in more non-Tibetans and therefore exacerbate Tibetan hostility towards China and Chinese. In a sense, since Beijing could not solve the Tibet Question by inducing the Dalai Lama to return and solidify its control of Tibet, it sought to do so without him by modernizing and developing Tibet while allowing its people the freedom to express their culture and practice their religion (within the limits of China's legal system).

Nevertheless, Beijing was unwilling to cut off discussions with the Dalai Lama, and a second face-to-face meeting between Tibetan representatives and China was held in Beijing in 1984. At this meeting, the Tibetans came with a developed negotiating position. They stated that the Dalai Lama rejected the Chinese five-point proposal and made their own substantive proposal that included creation of a demilitarized Greater Tibet with complete internal political autonomy.[12] It was, of course, futile from the start. Beijing was not willing to discuss real political autonomy for Tibet. It was looking to enhance its stability and security in Tibet, not lessen it by turning over political control of Tibet to its "enemies" in Dharamsala, let alone give them control over a Greater Tibet. In one sense, Dharamsala's leaders had misjudged both their own leverage and Beijing's desire for an agreement; in another sense, they simply could not bring themselves to contemplate accepting anything less. They were angry and frustrated by Chinese intransigence, and emotionally unable to believe that they could live under the rule of the Chinese Communist party. In this strained atmosphere a proposed visit of the Dalai Lama to China and Tibet fell by the wayside.

China continued to implement its internal policy, and by late 1985 to early 1986, many cadre and intellectuals believed that Beijing would soon initiate a second wave of reforms to fulfill the enhanced autonomous status implied by Hu Yaobang's statements. Under this system most officials would be ethnic Tibetans and the language of government would be Tibetan. In addition, the newly appointed head of the party in Tibet, Wu Jinghua, was himself a minority (from the Yi nationality) rather than a Han Chinese, sending the message that a Tibetan could be the next first secretary of the CCP. Wu Jinghua immediately began to make symbolic gestures showing his and the government's respect for Tibetan culture, for example, by wearing Tibetan dress on holidays. He also created an atmosphere of support for the development of Tibetan language and culture. Consequently, there was a feeling of possibility in the air in Lhasa, at least among Tibetan officials and intellectuals. This was still China to be sure, and political freedom of expression and assembly as we know them in the West were not permitted there or in the rest of China, but great strides had been made in permitting Tibetan culture and religion to flourish in a region that was still overwhelmingly Tibetan in demographic composition. Tibetans in exile were visiting Tibet in increasing numbers despite having to get visas as "overseas Chinese," and most resident Tibetans who went abroad to visit relatives returned.

However, another current was gaining momentum in China as Hu Yaobang's liberal approach came under attack with regard to China itself as well as to Tibet where more left-ist Tibetan and Chinese cadre were convinced that the policy of making greater concessions to Tibetans' ethnic sensitivity was flawed and dangerous. These senior officials tried to ob-struct Wu Jinghua's program in Tibet and criticized his ac-tions in Beijing through personal lines of communication. Nevertheless, the party's Tibet policy continued basically unchanged even after Hu Yaobang was forced to resign in January 1987.

Dharamsala, therefore, found itself in an awkward situa-tion. It was clear that Beijing had no intention of allowing Tibet a different political system, let alone independence. It was also clear that Beijing was enjoying some success in the sense that its reforms had the potential to win, if not the hearts of Tibetans, at least their stomachs. Material life had improved tremendously in both Lhasa and in the countryside where communes had been disbanded. At the same time, China's eco-nomic power and international prestige were increasing, a major goal of U.S. policy in Asia being to strengthen its strate-gic relationship with Beijing. Thus, there was now a real dan-ger that the exile's role in the Tibet Question would be mar-ginalized.

Dharamsala and the Dalai Lama responded in 1986–1987 by launching a new political offensive—what we can think of as their "international campaign."[13] It sought, on the one hand, to secure new Western political and economic leverage to force Beijing to offer the concessions they wanted, and on the other hand, to give Tibetans in Tibet the hope that the Dalai Lama was on the verge of securing Western assistance to settle the Tibet Question, in essence, shifting their attention from their stomachs to their ethnic hearts.

DHARAMSALA'S NEW INITIATIVE

The U.S. government was central to this new campaign. Of all the Western democracies, the United States had provided the most support for Tibetans during the difficult times of the 1950s and 1960s. However, when the United States jettisoned its containment strategy in favor of détente with China, direct support for Tibet ended. The Tibet issue was no longer even marginally important to U.S. national interests. The exile's new campaign, therefore, sought to regain active U.S. support by working through the soft underbelly of U.S. foreign policy—Congress. The key innovation in this strategy was having the Dalai Lama for the first time carry the exile's political message to the United States and Europe, particularly at governmental forums. Previously, he had traveled and spoken only as a religious leader.[14] With the help of Western supporters and donors and sympathetic U.S. representatives and congressional aides, a campaign was launched to gain American support for the exile's cause, in essence, to redirect the significance of the Tibet Question from the arena of geopolitical national interests to the sphere of core U.S. values—to the U.S. ideological commitment to freedom and human rights. The goal was to create a momentum that would lead the United States to support Tibet because it was the just and right thing for freedom-loving Americans to do.

In 1987 several major breakthroughs occurred. In June, the House of Representatives adopted a bill that condemned human rights abuses in Tibet, instructed the president to express sympathy for Tibet, and urged China to establish a constructive dialogue with the Dalai Lama.[15] Then on September 21, the Dalai Lama made his first political speech in America before the U.S. Congressional Human Rights Caucus. It was a carefully crafted and powerful talk arguing that Tibet had been independent when China invaded.[16] That invasion began what the Dalai Lama called China's illegal occupation of the country. Specifically, he said, "though Tibetans lost their freedom, under international law Tibet today is still an independent state under illegal occupation." The speech also raised serious human rights charges, referring twice to a Chinese-inflicted "holocaust" on the Tibetan people.

The Dalai Lama made a five-point proposal for solving the Tibet Question that called for the following:

1. Transforming Tibet into a "Zone of Peace"—this would include ethnographic Tibet and would require the withdrawal of all Chinese troops and military installations.

2. Reversing the population transfer policy which he said threatened the very existence of the Tibetans as a people.

3. Respecting the Tibetan people's fundamental human rights and democratic freedoms—it asserted that "deprived of all basic democratic rights and freedoms, [Tibetans] exist under a colonial administration in which all real power is wielded by Chinese officials of the Communist Party and the army."

4. Restoring and protecting Tibet's natural environment and abandoning China's use of Tibet for the production of nuclear weapons and dumping of nuclear waste.

5. Beginning earnest negotiations on the future status of Tibet and of relations between the Tibetan and Chinese peoples.

This speech was well received in the United States, and three weeks later, on October 6, the Senate passed its version of the earlier House bill. Ultimately, on December 22, 1987,

President Reagan signed the (1988–1989) Foreign Relations Authorization Act into law, including a nonbinding sense-of-the-Congress amendment that made the following points:

(i)   The United States should express sympathy for those Tibetans who have suffered and died as a result of fighting, persecution, or famine over the past four decades.

(ii) The United States should make the treatment of the Tibetan people an important factor in its conduct of relations with the People's Republic of China.

(iii) The Government of the People's Republic of China should respect internationally recognized human rights and end human rights violations against Tibetans.

(iv) The United States should urge the Government of the People's Republic of China to actively reciprocate the Dalai Lama's efforts to establish a constructive dialogue on the future of Tibet.

(viii) The United States should urge the People's Republic of China to release all political prisoners in Tibet.[17]

It also added a proviso that in regard to the sale of defense articles, the United States should take into consideration "the extent to which the Government of the People's Republic of China is acting in good faith and in a timely manner to resolve human rights issues in Tibet," and it authorized no less than fifteen scholarships to enable Tibetans to attend college in the United States.[18]

Although this policy was far weaker than the now-defunct position stated by Christian Herter in 1960, and it was only a "sense of Congress," it was seen in Dharamsala as a major victory—as the start of a Congress-driven move to create a new U.S. foreign policy that would proactively seek settlement of the Tibet Question in a manner favorable to the Dalai Lama. From out of nowhere, therefore, the United States was again actively involved in the Tibet Question, albeit through Congress rather than the executive branch or the State Department.

THE FIRST RIOT—OCTOBER 1, 1987

These activities of the Dalai Lama in the United States were widely known and eagerly followed in Lhasa.[19] Tibetans regularly listened to the Voice of America and BBC Chinese language broadcasts, and the Chinese government also broadcast attacks on the Dalai Lama's visit in the local media. On September 27, less than a week after the Dalai Lama's first speech in Washington, nationalistic monks from Drepung monastery in Lhasa staged a political demonstration in support of Tibetan independence and the Dalai Lama's initiative. They began by walking around the Inner Circle Road (*bagor*) that is both a main circumambulation route (going around the holy Lhasa Cathedral) and the main Tibetan market area. When no police appeared after several circuits, they marched down a main road to the offices of the Tibetan government. There they were arrested.

Four days later, on the morning of October 1, another group of twenty to thirty monks demonstrated in Lhasa to show their support for the Dalai Lama and the previous demonstrators, and to demand the latter's release from jail. Police quickly took them into custody and started beating them. A crowd of Tibetans who had gathered outside the police headquarters demanded these monks be released, and before long, this popular protest escalated into a full-scale riot. In the end, the police station and a number of vehicles and shops were burnt down, and anywhere from six to twenty Tibetans were killed when police (some of whom were ethnic Tibetans) fired at the crowds.

Beijing was shocked by the riot and the anti-Chinese anger it expressed. Clandestine nationalistic incidents had occurred for years in Lhasa but these were small, isolated activities that were easy to deal with. Now Beijing had to face the reality that thousands upon thousands of average Tibetans were angry enough to face death and prison by participating in a massive riot against the government and Chinese rule. This riot was particularly galling to Beijing because it coincided with the attacks of the Dalai Lama and U.S. congressional representatives, apparently proving to the world that statements about the horrendous conditions in Tibet were true despite the fact that the Chinese felt they were pursuing a moderate, conciliatory policy.

The months after the riots in Lhasa saw more demonstrations by monks and nuns and a steady stream of antigovernment posters. Nevertheless, the police were able to arrest the demonstrators quickly without provoking a riot. A cat-and-mouse game developed in which nationalistic monks launched demonstrations and the government tried to arrest them in a manner that would prevent another riot, for it was clearly the riot that had caught world attention, not simply the small demonstrations.

As 1987 drew to a close, attention in Lhasa turned to the coming Tibetan New Year in February 1988 and the accompanying Great Prayer Festival when almost 2,000 monks would come to Lhasa's Central Cathedral for several weeks of joint prayers.[20] The question of the day became whether the Prayer Festival would go on as planned, and if so, whether the monks would try to use it to launch a major demonstration. The risk of another riot was considerable since there would be thousands upon thousands of religious Tibetans in Lhasa at this time to witness the festival.

Many senior cadre in Tibet felt that the 1987 riot vindicated their contention that the conciliatory "ethnic" approach was dangerous and could result in the CCP losing power in Tibet. Several ad hoc secret meetings held in Lhasa and Chengdu (Sichuan) issued reports critical of the liberal policy and informally forwarded them to Beijing, where the new head of the party, Zhao Ziyang, convened a meeting of the larger Politburo to discuss Tibet. In November, its members decided that part of the present problem in Tibet was that Beijing's Tibet policy had not been properly carried out. However, at the same time, it also concluded that the policy had been too liberal. This marked the beginning of Beijing's retreat from its earlier approach.

Soon after the Politburo decision, the Lhasa daily newspaper announced the new line in a front-page article that laid part of the blame for the October riot on the excessive and incorrect application of "ultraleftist ideology" by local cadre. Until then it had totally blamed outside agitation for the demonstrations and riot. Now it admitted that its own officials were part of the problem. This was a calculated attempt to gain favor with the Tibetans in Lhasa by being realistic and forthright, even though the admission certainly angered many senior officials in Tibet.

At this time Beijing also made a decision that, in retrospect, was ill conceived. On the defensive internationally, the Chinese leadership apparently felt it was important to show the world that its liberal Tibetan religious policy was working, so it pushed ahead with the Great Prayer Festival. Wu Jinghua, the head of the TAR, announced that just as he had come to the Prayer Festival in Tibetan dress in the past, he would do so again this coming year to publicly show his respect for Tibetans' strong feelings about their religion and culture. He also announced that his three main priorities for Tibet were religion, national culture, and united front activities, in essence indicating that the core of his program would continue to be improved relations with Tibetans by paying attention to their ethnic sensitivities rather than to economic development per se.

The main event in this attempted reconciliation was a visit to Lhasa in early 1988 by the late Panchen Lama, Tibet's number-two incarnation. He was sent to Tibet with authorization to make concessions that would calm the monks and ensure the success of the Great Prayer Festival. The plan was to offer the monks substantial financial reparations and looser restrictions if they attended the Prayer Festival and in the future concentrated on religion, not politics. In response to demands that all monks be released before the festival, the Tibetan government on January 26, 1988, released fifty-nine monks as a gesture of goodwill, leaving only about fifteen monks in custody.[21] On the following day, at a big meeting at Drepung monastery, the Panchen Lama told the assembled monks that the government was willing to give 2 million yuan ($500,000) in reparations to the three Lhasa monasteries (Drepung, Sera, and Ganden).

The Panchen Lama's attempt to defuse the situation was unsuccessful. The anger of most of the monks toward Chinese policies in Tibet was too great to be assuaged by money. They felt that the Chinese were now trying to use the Prayer Festival as propaganda against the Dalai Lama's initiative, and they felt that time was on their side since the Dalai Lama was now succeeding in gaining U.S. support. Given this atmosphere, many of the older monks advised the government not to hold the Prayer Festival in Lhasa since they could not guarantee what the younger monks would do. They strongly recommended that the 1988 Prayer Festival be conducted at their own monasteries rather than in the Central Cathedral in Lhasa.

But the government dug in its heels and insisted the Great Prayer Festival had to go on. Foreign journalists had been invited, so the government cajoled, threatened, and pleaded with the monks to appear. Although many monks boycotted the event, most came and all went well until March 5, 1988, the last day. As the monks completed the procession of carrying the statue of Chamba (Maitreya), a monk shouted at the ranking officials seated at the ceremony to release a monk who remained in jail. When a Tibetan official told him to shut up, he and other monks immediately responded that Tibet is an independent country. Just when everyone thought that the ceremony had passed without a disaster, the situation went out of control and the latent anger exploded into the second terrible riot in Lhasa. Arrests and a clampdown in Tibet followed that further drew the mass of people to the side of the radical nationalists.

ETIOLOGY OF THE RIOTS

It is instructive to examine why the series of riots occurred if China was pursuing what it considered a moderate, ethnically sensitive reform policy.

The Chinese claim that the demonstration was in part inspired by Dharamsala. It is not clear whether Dharamsala (or other exile elements) actually asked one or more of the Drepung monastery monks to organize a demonstration, but it is clear that the monks' demonstration was meant to counter Chinese criticisms broadcast in the Lhasa media and demonstrate support for the Dalai Lama's new initiative in the United States. To this day the monks are proud that they risked (and are risking) their lives to support the Dalai Lama's efforts in the West on Tibet's behalf.[22]

One factor underlying the Tibetans' attitude was that they interpreted U.S. events in the framework of the Chinese system of government. In China, delegates at the People's Congress rubber-stamp what has already been decided by the party, so it was natural for Tibetans in Lhasa to believe that the support shown by members of the U.S. Congress reflected support by the U.S. *government* for the Dalai Lama and Tibetan independence. Many average Tibetans in Lhasa, therefore, believed that the Dalai Lama's speech to the Human Rights Caucus of Congress was a turning point in Tibetan history, and that the United States, in their eyes the world's greatest military power, would soon force China to "free" Tibet. Events in the West are well-known through shortwave radio broadcasts and play an important role in determining the attitude of Tibetans, particularly Lhasans.

In any case, it is clear that those first monk demonstrators never dreamed their civil disobedience in support of the Dalai Lama would provoke a bloody anti-Chinese riot. The real cause of the massive riot—as distinct from the small political demonstration—is complex. Despite the Chinese reforms, a volatile residue of bitterness and resentment against the government (which in Tibetans' minds was synonymous with the Han Chinese) remained.

Tibetans were still very angry about the loss of their country and the personal and collective (ethnic) suffering they had experienced since 1959 under direct Chinese rule. Like some minority groups in the United States, they view past oppression as part of present reality and direct their resentment at today's Han Chinese. The condescending attitudes of many Han in Tibet tended to reinforce these ill feelings.

Moreover, Chinese insistence on a crash program of economic development in Tibet created new problems, the most important of which was the large influx of Chinese and Muslims (Han and Hui) into Tibet since 1984. Ironically, this process does not appear to have started as a deliberate Chinese scheme to "swamp" Tibet with Han "colonists," as is often charged, but rather as a result of the government's desire to develop Tibet quickly. The large funds disbursed for development projects created a substantial economic ripple effect, attracting thousands of Han construction workers whose presence in turn created a demand for scores of new Chinese restaurants, shops, and services. This, however, was understood to be problematic, and the party secretary in Tibet at one time in 1984 actually stopped Han and Hui coming in from Qinghai. But the larger need in Tibet for carpenters, masons, and other skilled workers gradually overwhelmed these attempts, and the success of these Han tradesmen and craftsmen sent a message to the surrounding provinces that there was profit to be made in Tibet, drawing in even larger numbers of new Han and Hui annually. Today even Han beggars ply their trade in Lhasa. Most Tibetans in Lhasa resented the increasing control of the Han in their local economy, taking jobs away from them and Sinicizing their beloved city. They wanted economic improvement but not at the expense of transforming the ethnic and demographic character of Lhasa and Tibet.

The accelerated development program for Tibet therefore exacerbated existing local feelings of anger and bitterness over past harms done to Tibet since "liberation" in 1951, and worked to undermine the positive impact of the new reforms on Tibetans' attitudes and feelings. Moreover, it focused Tibetans' attention precisely on the volatile ethnic or national issue— there were too many Han in Tibet and they were getting too many benefits. This situation in turn fueled the Tibetans' feeling of powerlessness and abuse at the hands of the dominant Han.

Another important problem was Beijing's reluctance to permit as full an expression of cultural and religious freedom as Tibetans wanted. Although a substantial revival of Buddhism had occurred since Deng's rise to power, and many once-great monasteries like Drepung were again functioning as genuine religious centers, a number of restrictions in areas such as the total number of monks remained. These limits angered the monks and many laymen and highlighted the fact that Tibetans are still beholden to an alien, Chinese value system for permission to practice their own religion and culture in their own homeland. From Beijing's perspective, however, these restrictions made sense since the monasteries were hotbeds of nationalism and proindependence activists. Allowing them to grow in size and wealth would strengthen the very people who were most dedicated to challenging China's position in Tibet, but restricting them made it easy for Tibetans in Lhasa to see the glass as half empty rather than half full.

Finally, one cannot underestimate the strong historical and nationalistic sense of Tibet as an exclusively Tibetan homeland. Because there were *no* Han Chinese in Tibet in 1950, all adult Tibetans vividly remember a completely Tibetan Tibet. They felt that the Chinese had taken their country and were transforming it into just another part of China. They believed (and believe) that Tibet should be run by Tibetans, use Tibetan language, and follow laws that are in accordance with the deeply felt values and beliefs at the heart of Tibetan culture. For most Tibetans, the new reforms had made progress toward that end, but it was not enough for individuals to be allowed to turn prayer wheels and burn butter lamps if Tibet were not a homogeneous ethnic entity. The influx of Han workers was clearly a serious a step in the wrong direction, and was not in keeping with the spirit of Hu Yaobang's policy.

In the fall of 1987, on the eve of the first riot, Lhasa's Tibetans therefore had ambivalent attitudes and feelings. Pent-up anger, resentment, and frustration competed with the realization that cultural, linguistic, and economic conditions had improved dramatically. And critically, the new successes of the Dalai Lama in the United States offered what seemed a realistic alternative to Chinese domination—it gave them new hope that with the work of the Dalai Lama and the power of the United States, independence was just around the corner.

In this atmosphere the quintessential symbol of Tibetan civilization and greatness—the monks—provided the catalyst needed to ignite the anger. The 1987 and 1988 riots were thus primarily spontaneous outbursts of pent-up resentment and anger. Rather than a rejection of the reform policy since 1980, they were unplanned responses to a situation that Tibetans felt symbolized the loss of their nationhood and the denigration of their culture since 1959 by a dominant and alien group. They share many similarities with the terrible racial riots the United States experienced in Watts and other inner-city neighborhoods, or the anger of Native Americans that exploded at Wounded Knee. When Tibetans saw the police beating up the unarmed monks, they responded with their ethnic hearts. They responded not to poor material conditions, but to past injustices and to present domination by an alien majority.

Building one more stadium, or road, or factory, or apartment building could no more eliminate that problem in Lhasa than it could in the U.S. ghettos.

BEIJING'S HARD-LINE STRATEGY

New congressional support in the United States, coupled with the demonstrations and riots in Tibet, led the exiles to conclude that they were beginning to amass the critical leverage needed to pressure Beijing to yield to their demands for political autonomy.

In April of 1988, the Chinese announced that if the Dalai Lama publicly gave up the goal of independence, he could live in Tibet (rather than Beijing). Two months later, on June 15, 1988, the Dalai Lama responded to this announcement in an address to the European Parliament at Strasbourg. This marked the first public statement of his conditions for returning to Tibet. Its main points were:

> The whole of Tibet [political and ethnographic] . . . should become a self-governing democratic political entity founded on law by agreement of the people for the common good and protection of themselves and their environment, in association with the People's Republic of China.
>
> The Government of the People's Republic of China could remain responsible for Tibet's foreign policy. The Government of Tibet should, however, develop and maintain relations through its own Foreign Affairs Bureau, in the fields of religion, commerce, education, culture, tourism, science, sports, and other nonpolitical activities. Tibet should join international organizations concerned with such activities.
>
> The Government of Tibet should be founded on a constitution of basic law. The basic law should provide for a democratic system of government . . . This means that the Government of Tibet will have the right to decide on all affairs relating to Tibet and Tibetans.
>
> As individual freedom is the real source and potential of any society's development, the Government of Tibet would seek to

ensure this freedom by adherence to the Universal Declaration of Human Rights, including the rights to speech, assembly, and religion. Because religion constitutes the source of Tibet's national identity, and spiritual values lie at the very heart of Tibet's rich culture, it would be the special duty of the Government of Tibet to safeguard and develop its practice.

The Government should be comprised of a popularly elected Chief Executive, a bi-cameral legislative branch, and an independent judicial system. Its seat should be Lhasa.

The social and economic system of Tibet should be determined in accordance with the wishes of the Tibetan people, bearing in mind especially the need to raise the standard of living of the entire population.

. . . A regional peace conference should be called to ensure Tibet becomes a genuine sanctuary of peace through demilitarization. Until such a peace conference can be convened and demilitarized and neutralization achieved, China could have the right to maintain a restricted number of military installations in Tibet. These must be solely for defense purposes.[23]

The Dalai Lama indicated he was ready to talk with the Chinese about this proposal and announced the membership of his negotiating team, including a Dutch national as its legal advisor.

The Strasbourg proposal did not seek complete independence, but it also did not accept the limited autonomy of the Chinese political system. Rather it called for Tibet to have a new status as a kind of autonomous dominion much as it had been under the Qing dynasty. The Dalai Lama would accept being part of China, but China would have little authority over affairs in Tibet. Since this proposal had in essence been presented to Beijing at the secret 1984 talks, it did not represent anything new to the Chinese. Nevertheless, the speech was important because it was the first time the Dalai Lama openly told his people (and the world) that independence was not a realistic goal and that he was willing to accept Tibet as part of China if it could be totally autonomous. It was in this sense a courageous initiative, and it created a stir in exile politics, where it was criticized by many as a sellout.[24]

The proposal was also an effective political tactic. If, as the exile leaders hoped, their victories had persuaded Beijing to view this level of political autonomy more favorably now than in 1984, serious negotiations could have ensued. At the same time, it placed Beijing in a difficult situation since Deng Xiaoping and other top leaders had repeatedly said that with the exception of independence they would discuss anything. Now the Dalai Lama had given them just such an opportunity before the eyes of the world. Consequently, rejection would make Beijing seem unreasonable and simultaneously enhance the Dalai Lama's international reputation as a statesman willing to compromise in order to attain a lasting peace.

The Strasbourg address initially threw Beijing into confusion. The leadership had not changed its basic view of what compromise solution it was willing to accept, but there was support for at least giving the impression of willingness to discuss the Strasbourg proposal since it did not demand independence per se. Ultimately, after some initial signs of interest, the more hard-line view predominated and Strasbourg was rejected as an indirect form of independence. In retrospect, given the internal situation in China, it is difficult to see how Beijing could have permitted Tibetans to have the freedoms associated with Western democracies and not offer the rest of China the same options, let alone how it could allow the creation of a Greater Tibet. It was also unnecessarily provocative for Dharamsala to include a Western advisor on the negotiating team given China's feelings about outside interference. Talks, therefore, did not occur and six months later, in December 1988, monks demonstrating in commemoration of International Human Rights Day precipitated a third bloody riot in Lhasa.

In the midst of this deteriorating situation the unexpected death on January 28, 1989, of Tibet's second highest incarnation—the Panchen Lama—produced a surprising secret initiative from Beijing. Hoping to cut through the impasse with the Dalai Lama, China had its Buddhist Association invite the Dalai Lama to Beijing to participate in the memorial ceremony for the Panchen Lama, letting it be known that this would be a good time for him to discuss the political situation informally with top Chinese officials.[25] The Dalai Lama had suddenly been offered an exceptional opportunity to visit China without having to sort out complicated political protocol issues. The rationale behind this approach was the belief in China that the Dalai Lama was more moderate than his advisors and direct discussion might possibly break the deadlock.

The Dalai Lama and his officials, however, were reluctant to accept the invitation. The Chinese had indicated that the Dalai Lama would not be allowed to visit Tibet, so the exile leaders were concerned that Tibetans in Lhasa might feel abandoned if he went to China but not Tibet. They also feared that China might humiliate the Dalai Lama by ignoring him or treating him as a minor figure. Additionally, it is also likely that hardline officials in Dharamsala feared that in face-to-face talks with top Chinese leaders the Dalai Lama might accept a less favorable compromise than they wanted. So, with events apparently going well from their perspective, the exile leadership persuaded the Dalai Lama to take the safe course and decline the invitation, telling the Chinese Buddhist Association that they had done all the appropriate rites in Dharamsala.[26] Many look back at this as one of the most important lost opportunities in the post-1978 era.

Meanwhile, the situation in Tibet deteriorated further in 1989. Tibetans in Lhasa continued to mount small nationalistic demonstrations, one of which turned into the fourth Lhasa riot on March 5, 1989. At this juncture, Beijing accepted the fact that Tibet was veering out of control and initiated strong measures

1. Despite being educated government office workers, this couple, as is common in Tibet, opted for a traditional Tibetan wedding. Hundreds of invited guests filed by the groom (left) and bride (right) in this tiny room, draping a traditional Tibetan ceremonial scarf (*katak*) on each of their necks and leaving a cash present in a Tibetan (hand-folded) envelope on the table in front of them. The guests then retired to a large rented hall where they were feted for each of the next three days— drinking, eating, and playing games like *mah-jongg*.

2. Ringed by the bare hills of the Lhasa Valley, the inner city—the old section of town where most of the indigenous Lhasans live—is a jumble of streets shared by cars, bikes, rickshaws, and pedestrians. Most of the traditional houses lining the street have been replaced with concrete buildings, but generally—as seen in this photograph—in a similar style. The ubiquitous prayer flags fluttering on the roofs signal Tibetans' strong commitment to their traditional religion and culture.

3. For a thousand years, Tibetan monks and laypersons have gone on pilgrimages to holy sites throughout Tibet. Many walk for months to remote places like Mt. Kailash, the famous center of the Buddhist universe located in far western Tibet where this lone monk was headed. Carrying his belongings on a traditional bentwood rucksack frame and clutching the classic wooden pilgrim's staff in his hand, he had already traveled five months (over seven hundred miles from his home monastery in Sichuan province) to reach this *stupa* two hundred miles west of Lhasa. And he still had another three hundred fifty miles (two months) to walk to reach his goal.

4.–5. Left—A family of nomads from northern Tibet on pilgrimage in Lhasa to see the famous Jo Rimpoche statue in Lhasa's cathedral. Dressed in their everyday nomad sheepskin clothes, this was their first visit to Lhasa. Right—By contrast, these two Lhasa Tibetans are chic and modern and would not have seemed out of place in Beijing or Cleveland. Beijing's hope is that this generation (and their children) will become modern Tibetans, comfortable with being part of China.

6. A nomad girl living at an altitude of 16,500 feet on Tibet's "Changtang" (northern plateau), carefully examines her "make-up" in a mirror manufactured in eastern China. The rouge on her cheeks is actually from a seal-stamping inkpad.

7. Students at a village primary school in Drigung county start the day with a round of calisthenics. For many families in this area, school represents a hope that some of their children will be able to find work off the family farm.

8. One of the most popular holiday periods in Lhasa is *Shodün,* the festival of the traditional Tibetan opera that is performed in late August. The plays have Buddhist themes and are performed by masked dancer-singers. Thousands of Lhasans attend the performances in Drepung monastery, Norbulingka, and other locations around Lhasa. Here the *ngomba,* or "hunters," were performing their dance.

9. The birthday of the fourteenth Dalai Lama (July 6) is a holiday in Lhasa celebrated by thousands of Tibetans going to a park in the southeastern part of the city, offering propitiations in the form of prayers, incense, and barley-flour, and having picnics. In recent years a new custom has emerged in which everyone attending throws roasted barley-flour at one another. After an hour of this, all the participants are covered from head to foot with white flour.

10. One area of economic development where Tibetans have been able to excel is the production and export of hand-knotted carpets. Tibetans have adapted the designs and production techniques of their traditional carpet making to produce internationally competitive rugs. Here two young women employed by a large co-op carpet factory in Lhasa work on a huge loom weaving a livingroom-size rug.

11. Many Chinese itinerant peddlers like this man walk the streets of Lhasa selling sunglasses to local Tibetans like this boy.

12. Chinese involvement in Tibet's economy now includes beggars and manual laborers like this Han Chinese man.

13. Tibetans in Lhasa throw some incense into a fire along the five-mile circumambulation road that circuits the city. Each of the women turns a hand-held prayer wheel throughout the circumambulation.

14. After being totally eliminated during the Cultural Revolution, monastic life has been revived throughout Tibet, although the largest monastery in Lhasa, Drepung, now holds only seven hundred where it held ten thousand in 1959. Here a young monk sits in his apartment in Drepung monastery memorizing a religious text.

15. Education has become increasingly important in Lhasa, and private pre-primary schools have become popular with many parents. This school was founded and operated by a former monk official in the traditional government and had several score of students learning how to read and write in Tibetan. Here an older student helps teach a new preschooler how to write in Tibetan using the old custom of holding the student's hand and moving it through the motions of forming the letter.

16. Police and army in Lhasa generally keep a low profile until there is a political disturbance. Here some police monitor a major road in the west of Lhasa. The monument in the background honors the Chinese workers who built the main road from China to Lhasa in the 1950s. In 1996 it was damaged by a bomb placed by Tibetan nationalists.

to quell the unrest, taking the drastic step of declaring martial law in Tibet.

The year 1989 brought another dramatic setback for Beijing when the Dalai Lama was awarded the Nobel Peace Prize. Tibetans everywhere considered this a major victory—an indirect but powerful statement that their cause was just and valid, and a sign that the world was lining up behind the Dalai Lama in his fight with China. Finally, 1989 also brought the Tiananmen debacle. Although this event had no direct impact on the situation in Tibet because Tibetans had little interest in or sympathy for what they considered a "Han" affair, it fostered a more hardline political policy in China that made it easier to take stern measures in Tibet.

By the end of 1989, therefore, Beijing's internal and external strategies for Tibet were clearly in shambles. Unless China was willing to relinquish direct political control in Tibet and accept a Strasbourg-like dominion status, the exiles appeared bent on continuing their international campaign, thus encouraging more internal demonstrations and new international accusations. Momentum appeared to have shifted to the Dalai Lama, whose international initiative had successfully turned the tables on China, placing Beijing on the defensive both in the world arena and within Tibet.

Beijing reacted predictably to the threat this shift in momentum posed by moving to a more hard-line, integrationist policy. In Beijing it was hard for moderates to refute the historical parallel between Mao's gradualist Tibet policy (supporting the Dalai Lama while postponing reforms), precipitating the 1959 rebellion, and Hu Yaobang's policy, leading to the 1987–1989 riots. Many officials felt strongly that if China did not stop "coddling" the reactionary and superstitious Tibetans, matters could get completely out of hand. A comment made by Qiao Shi, China's security chief (now head of the National People's Congress) during an investigative trip to Lhasa reveals the anger and frustration felt in Beijing. At a Tibetan

Political Consultative Conference meeting in Lhasa, former Tibetan government and religious leaders criticized current policy on religion, language, and economics. Qiao Shi responded angrily, lashing out at the former elite in "class struggle" language they hadn't heard since the rise of Deng Xiaoping in 1978. He reminded them that the government had made monetary restitutions for its past wrongs and gave them a new high status; then he sarcastically asked whether they wanted still more—"What do you want us to do?" he said, "Give you back your servants so that you can live like the old society?"

The move away from the moderate Hu Yaobang approach was formalized in the winter of 1989 at a meeting of the Politburo. The general feeling among the leadership was that the measures Beijing had taken to liberalize conditions within Tibet had neither produced greater appreciation from the Lhasan masses nor convinced them that their interests could best be met as part of China. To the contrary, they had increased nationalistic aspirations and had yielded disturbances and riots that actually weakened China's position in Tibet. This failure prompted Beijing to focus on a strategy to enhance their security in Tibet in ways that did not depend on having to win over the large segment of Tibet's current adult generation who were considered hopelessly reactionary.

The new policy operated under the assumption that it was unrealistic to expect the Dalai Lama to play a constructive role in Tibet. Beijing would try to solve the Tibetan problem without him. More concretely, the leadership of the party in Tibet was to be strengthened by sending better educated personnel (non-Tibetans) who would be able to modernize the area and people more effectively. Similarly, greater emphasis was placed on educating young Tibetan cadre and reinvigorating the party structure at all levels—from the top down to the village level. And, of course, security was vastly improved by increasing the number of plainclothes officers and police substations in volatile areas and enhancing surveillance equipment. As a result of these and other measures, new demonstrations were quickly brought under control and prevented from escalating into riots. Indeed, during the seven years since martial law was lifted in 1990, there have been no new riots, despite frequent demonstrations. This control was accomplished, moreover, without restricting the day-to-day life of the inhabitants of Lhasa—as long as Lhasans did not engage in political dissidence, they were free to go where they wished, meet with friends, invite monks for religious services, have parties, and so forth. This success has given Beijing's leaders confidence that their security forces can handle whatever tactics Tibetans dissidents (or exiles) employ.

The cornerstone of the central government's new policy was (and is) economic growth and modernization—accelerating economic development in Tibet by providing large subsidies for development projects aimed at building infrastructure and productive capacity. This strategy seeks to modernize Tibet's economy and people, increasing their income and reducing their isolation by inextricably linking Tibet's economy with the rest of China. To do this effectively, Beijing has decided that Tibet must be rapidly developed. The Third (National) Tibet Work Conference held in Beijing in July 1994, for example, decreed that Tibet "urgently needs to develop faster" and set out an economic program that called for 10 percent economic growth per annum and a doubling of Tibet's 1993 gross domestic product by the year 2000. Beijing also has committed 2.38 billion yuan (about 270 million dollars) for sixty-two infrastructure construction projects approved at the 1994 meeting.[27]

In some ways, the new economic strategy is doing what Beijing hoped. A number of Tibetans have clearly benefited economically, and others are now turning their attention from politics to new economic opportunities. However, the policy also appears to be creating a serious backlash.

A key component of the "economic integration" approach is the freedom of non-Tibetans (Han and Hui) to do business in Tibet. Tens of thousands of Han and Hui have been drawn to Tibet to participate in construction projects and to open businesses. These numbers are continuing to increase as Beijing escalates its economic funds and subsidies there. These non-Tibetans are part of a phenomenon common throughout China called "floating population"—that is to say, they are permanent residents in one area (usually a village) but live and work temporarily in another, usually a city. They do not have "citizen" rights in the place where they work, so they are not "colonists" in the usual sense, but nonetheless they live there for all or part of any given year.[28] Begun in earnest when China extended its "open door" policy to Tibet in 1984–1985, this influx has accelerated tremendously as a result of the rapid economic development. There are no accurate data on the numbers of such people in Tibet (TAR), but they have dramatically changed the demographic composition and atmosphere of Lhasa and are beginning to expand into smaller "urban" areas such as county seats (*xian*). The number of these non-Tibetans is unprecedented in Tibetan history and has turned Lhasa, the political heart of Tibet, into a city where non-Tibetan residents appear to equal or exceed the number of actual Tibetans.

Non-Tibetans now control a large segment of all levels of the local economy—from street corner bicycle repairmen to computer store owners to large firms trading with the rest of China. Numerous Tibetans in Lhasa have complained about this flood, arguing that it should be stopped or severely limited because Tibet is a minority "autonomous region" where Tibetans, not outsiders, should be the primary beneficiaries of the new growth in the market economy. Tibetans believe they cannot compete economically with the more skilled and industrious Han and Hui; without government intervention to ensure the welfare of the citizens of the autonomous region, they expect to become increasingly marginalized both economically and demographically.[29] These voices argue that just as Beijing has erected powerful barriers to keep more advanced foreigners from taking control of China's new industrial ventures, Tibet should adopt regulations that protect Tibetans from the more advantaged and better financed Chinese.

Beijing rejects this argument, insisting that rapid development takes precedence over all else. It has refused to stop or restrict the flow of non-Tibetan workers or to pass specific economic protection legislation for minority regions. Deng Xiaoping himself strongly supported this position. In 1987, for example, he said: "Tibet is sparsely populated. The two million Tibetans are not enough to handle the task of developing such a huge region. There is no harm in sending Han into Tibet to help. You cannot reach a proper conclusion if you base your assessment of ethnic policy and the Tibet Question on how many Han are in Tibet. The key issues are what is best for Tibetans and how can Tibet develop at a fast pace, and move ahead in the four modernizations in China."[30]

Beijing's reluctance to terminate this influx is, of course, also politically and strategically motivated. The large numbers of non-Tibetans living and working in Tibet provide Beijing a new and formidable pro-China "constituency" that increases its security there.[31] Although these Chinese do not see themselves as permanent colonists, at any given time a large number of ethnic Chinese reside in key urban areas in Tibet. And like Americans who end up living their lives in cities where they went to work for just a few years, many Han may end up living their lives in Tibet as well. Thus, since Beijing cannot now persuade the majority of Tibetans to ignore the Dalai Lama and accept that being part of China is in their best interests, it can allow large numbers of people for whom this is a given to live in Tibet. One can easily imagine that if China's control over Tibet became seriously threatened by militant violence, not only would more troops be rushed in, but new laws could be promulgated to make the large Han presence permanent by offering attractive perks to induce the "floating population" to accept permanent status in Tibet.

Equally important to China's leaders is the expectation that these Chinese will provide a powerful model of modern thinking and behavior that Tibetans will see and gradually emulate. Based on the history of other minority areas, Beijing's leaders are partially banking on a process of acculturation in which the more "advanced" Han will open up Tibetans to new ideas and attitudes and create a new, "modern" Tibetan in the process who will not be so influenced by religion and lamas. Thus, while Beijing realizes that its open-door policy will likely create much pain and anguish among Tibetans in the short run, it feels that this is the price it must pay for modernizing Tibetan society, and that in the long run it will triumph.

Many Tibetans, including Tibetan cadres and intellectuals, however, have been embittered by this policy. A "black" joke making the rounds of minority officials in Lhasa illustrates Tibetans' disappointment with China's policies:

> *Do you know the four periods of modern Tibetan history [under the PRC]?*
>
> In the first 10 years (1950–60) we lost our land [i.e., Chinese troops entered and took control of Tibet]; in the second ten years (1960–70) we lost political power [i.e., the traditional government was replaced by a Han-dominated Communist government]; in the third ten years (1970–80), we lost our culture [i.e., the Cultural Revolution destroyed religion and other old customs]; in the fourth ten years (1980–90), we lost our economy [i.e., the open door economic policy allowed non-Tibetans to dominate the autonomous region's economy].

Beijing is also trying to use the education system to create a "modern," better educated Tibetan elite. In addition to the standard school system in Tibet, a program of building special Tibetan middle schools in other parts of China began in 1985 and was expanded substantially after 1987. Today there are roughly 10,000 Tibetan youths attending such schools throughout the rest of China, and more also attend vocational schools. In 1994, another wave of educational and party reform was begun within Tibet that sought both to reduce illiteracy and to control more closely the content of education so that Tibetan students will not be exposed to subtle nationalist, separatist ideology. Similarly, in 1994 Tibet's government officials were ordered to recall any of their children who were attending school in Dharamsala and to cease keeping photographs of the Dalai Lama in their homes.[32]

Such measures are unlikely to eliminate ethnic loyalties and sentiments; for example, many Tibetan students living in inland China have their Tibetan identities reinforced when they encounter prejudice and bigotry at the hands of local Han. Nonetheless, these changes may in time create a category of better educated, less religious Tibetans who feel more comfortable living as part of Chinese society. It is too early to assess the likelihood of this.

Beijing's current "hard-line" Tibet policy extends to cultural issues such as language. While Tibetans are free to dress, speak, write, and live "Tibetan," Beijing is now reluctant to implement (institutionalize) additional "cultural" changes that would emphasize the distinctness of Tibet and isolate Tibet further from the rest of China. Thus, China is not implementing language reforms that would mandate Tibetan language as the standard for government offices, and it has been dragging its feet on expanding a program to teach science in Tibetan language in high school, despite the recent completion of a six-year trial program in which students in such programs performed better on college entrance exams than those in the normal Chinese-language science classes. And in early 1997 there were indications of an ominous reversal in Tibet's educational policy from expanding the use of the Tibetan language in schools to introducing Chinese language earlier.[33] Similarly, Beijing continues to limit

the number of monks and has tightened its control over re-
building monasteries and over the administration of existing
monasteries.

In essence, therefore, Beijing's post-1989 policy has implicitly
redefined what is meant by ethnic or cultural autonomy in
Tibet. Special subsidies and preferential treatment still exist in a
number of areas such as family planning, but the basic policy
has moved from the view that Tibet has a special status in
China because of its history to the view that Tibet is just another
ethnic group in a multiethnic state. Tibet is therefore seen as a
region in which Tibetans can practice and pass on their culture
if they wish, but without a special commitment to ensure that
demographic and linguistic homogeneity are perpetuated. The
"ethnic sensibility" approach has been displaced by a less conciliatory policy in which modernizing Tibet and creating a new
breed of "modern" Tibetan takes precedence. Measures that
make Tibet more distinct and separate from the rest of China,
therefore, are now rejected (or obstructed) as antithetical to
China's national interest. All of this, however, strikes at the
heart of Tibetans' nationalistic view of Tibet as the homeland of
their people and culture—their country. It highlights their continued powerlessness in relation to Han interests and intensifies
the bitter enmity many Tibetans feel toward Han Chinese and
the central government. Beijing has therefore embarked on a
high-risk strategy in Tibet that may very well backfire and exacerbate the very violence, bloodshed, and hatred it seeks to
overcome.

The hard-line strategy in Tibet has relegated the Dalai Lama
to the sidelines and is forcing him to watch events unfold that
are from his point of view tragic. For well over a thousand
years of recorded history, through wars and conquest, famines
and natural disasters, Tibet remained the exclusive home of a
people. Now Tibetans in Tibet and in exile see this being lost
right under their eyes. The Dalai Lama continues to experience
great international sympathy and has tremendous influence

over the attitudes of the local Tibetans in Tibet, but he has no leverage to stop China's new policy since it does not depend on winning the approval of local Tibetans (in the short run at least) and since the international community has not provided meaningful support.

Beijing has therefore turned the tables back on Dharamsala. The triumphs of the Dalai Lama's international campaign look more and more like pyrrhic victories. The international initiative won significant symbolic gains for the exiles in the West, but not only did it not compel China to yield to its demands, it played a major role in precipitating the new hard-line policy that is changing the nature of Tibet. Ironically, by threatening China's political hold over Tibet, Dharamsala and its Western supporters provided the advocates of a hard-line Tibet policy the leverage they needed to shift Beijing's Tibet policy away from the ethnically sensitive one advocated by Hu Yaobang in the early 1980s.

The Future

What of the future? How is this conflict likely to play out as we move into the twenty-first century? Is there any common ground on which to construct a reconciliation between the Dalai Lama and China? Does the United States have a role to play?

CHINA

Beijing now has little interest in new discussions with the Dalai Lama because it believes he still is not serious about making the kind of compromise China can accept. The 1995 controversy over the selection of a new Panchen Lama in China illustrates the enormous difficulty both sides have in compromising, as well as why Beijing has such misgivings about the Dalai Lama.

When the tenth Panchen Lama died in Tibet on January 28, 1989, the Chinese government agreed to permit the selection of a new Panchen Lama. Because they were atheists, it made no difference to the Communist party leaders which boy was ultimately chosen to be the new Panchen Lama, but since it did matter to Tibetans, the selection process would obviously need to adhere to Tibetan customs and norms to some degree in order to ensure that the new incarnation would be accepted as authentic and legitimate in Tibet. At the same time, Beijing considered it politically necessary that the search process unequivocally demonstrate its authority over the selection of reincarnations, and that the next Panchen Lama be found in China. Beijing's strategy for achieving these two goals was to constitute a "traditional" Tibetan search team composed of lamas and monk officials of the late Panchen Lama's monastery (Tashilhunpo) and empower them to employ customary methods (dreams, omens, signs, searches) to identify a set of incarnation "candidates." Once this was completed, a religious lottery would be held in which one of the candidates would be anonymously drawn from a "golden urn" under the supervision of the central government, which would then formally confirm and install the boy selected.[1] The custom of a golden urn lottery was begun by the Qing dynasty emperor Qian Long in 1792.

The problem with this plan was that Tibetan norms required that the new Panchen Lama be confirmed by the Dalai Lama, and Beijing's plan included no role for him. This was not surprising given the fact that the Dalai Lama rejected both the golden urn lottery and the authority of the Chinese government to approve or disapprove the final selection of Tibetan lamas; he, to the contrary, claimed that ultimate authority rested with him.[2] Consequently, while excluding the Dalai Lama from the selection process simplified the finding of a new Panchen Lama for Beijing (and reinforced its political claims), doing so was likely to result in the Dalai Lama rejecting the legitimacy of the Chinese-selected Panchen Lama and probably selecting a different Panchen Lama in exile. Consequently, the officials of the late Panchen Lama urged modification of the initial guidelines so that an attempt could be made to reach some arrangement with the Dalai Lama over the selection.

The Dalai Lama also appeared to want to prevent the selection of the next Panchen Lama from turning into a political circus. In March 1991, he sent a message to the Chinese embassy in New Delhi saying he would be willing to assist in the selection process, and from 1990 to 1993, his elder brother, Gyalo Thondup, urged the Chinese government on several occasions to involve the Dalai Lama by allowing him to send lamas to Tibet to assist in the search.[3]

China did not agree to this, but it did permit Tashilhunpo monastery's Chadrel Rimpoche, the head of the search team, to contact the Dalai Lama. On July 17, 1993, Chadrel Rimpoche took the occasion of a Gyalo Thondup visit to Beijing to give him a communiqué for the Dalai Lama.[4] Written in the old Tibetan scroll format and referring to the Dalai Lama with the most exalted titles, honorifics, and phraseologies, it asked for the Dalai Lama's prayers and help in attaining a speedy decision in the selection of the Panchen Lama; that is, it asked the Dalai Lama to cooperate in the selection process.[5] The Chinese attitude at this time seemed to be that it would be excellent if the Dalai Lama was willing to cooperate, but if he was not, China would continue without him.

Gyalo Thondup carried the letter to the Dalai Lama in India, but his response was tough, asking that Chadrel Rimpoche come to India for consultations.[6] Overtly this was not a negative response, but since internal politics in China would make such a visit impossible, it left ambiguous how far the Dalai Lama was willing to go to ensure that the next Panchen Lama would be chosen without political controversy. This response, which the Chinese publicly ignored, provided the hard-liners in China further evidence that it was futile to try to deal with the Dalai Lama.

Because it was critical from a Tibetan point of view that the Dalai Lama recognize the new Panchen Lama, Chadrel Rimpoche continued to communicate informally with the Dalai Lama. By the end of 1994 the search team had compiled the list of "candidates" from which the eleventh Panchen Lama would be chosen, and Chadrel Rimpoche sent the Dalai Lama a letter providing detailed information (including photographs)

on about twenty-five candidates. He also informed the Dalai
Lama that all signs indicated that one of these boys—Gendun
Choekyi Nyima—was the true incarnation.[7] The Dalai Lama
examined the evidence early in 1995 and agreed with Chadrel
Rimpoche's conclusion, despite the urging of some in India that
he order the Tashilhunpo monks in exile to search for the next
Panchen Lama outside of Tibet. By early February the Dalai
Lama got a message back to Chadrel Rimpoche stating that he
had done divination that confirmed Gendun Choekyi Nyima.

This was an important victory for Chadrel Rimpoche and
the officials who had urged that Tashilhunpo be permitted to
search for the reincarnation in accordance with Tibetan norms
and that the Dalai Lama be contacted. It now seemed certain
there would be only one Panchen Lama, found in China as
Beijing had initially mandated. All that was left was to work
out how to finalize the selection and announce the decision so
that neither the Dalai Lama nor Beijing lost face.[8] The selection of the previous Panchen Lama (which took place over the
years from 1941 to 1949) seemed to offer a model for such a
compromise.

Relations between the Panchen and Dalai Lamas in the early
twentieth century were poor, so when the thirteenth Dalai
Lama levied new taxes on feudal estate holders after his return
to Lhasa from India in 1913, the ninth Panchen Lama refused,
arguing that the terms of his land grants (from the Manchu emperor) precluded such additional taxation.[9] The thirteenth
Dalai Lama's insistence on payment precipitated the flight of
the ninth Panchen Lama into exile in China together with his
top officials in 1924. He died there in 1937.

In keeping with Tibetan tradition, the late Panchen Lama's
officials (those in exile in China) set about to find his incarnation. In 1941 they identified a Tibetan boy in Qinghai province
and decided he was the new Panchen Lama. The Dalai Lama,
however, refused to accept the boy found in Qinghai province,

instructing the Panchen Lama's entourage in China to send him to Lhasa for a final examination that would include two other candidates. When the late Panchen's officials objected, insisting they were positive their boy was the true incarnation, the Tibetan government withheld its final recognition of the Qinghai boy as the new Panchen Lama.

The Panchen Lama's officials in China meanwhile had also been seeking formal recognition of their selection from Chiang Kaishek's government, China having claimed ultimate authority over the selection of the Panchen and Dalai Lamas since the Qing dynasty.[10] After much deliberation, the Chinese government finally accepted the choice of the late Panchen's officials, in large part to persuade them to flee to Taiwan. On June 3, 1949, while the Nationalists were in the process of withdrawing from the mainland to Taiwan, Li Zongren, the acting president of the Chinese Nationalist government, formally recognized the Qinghai boy—who was then eleven years old[11]—and on August 10, 1949, an enthronement ceremony was held in Kumbum monastery in Qinghai province, attended by the head of the Chinese government's Commission for Mongolian and Tibetan Affairs (on behalf of Li Zongren). There were, of course, no officials from the Tibetan government in Lhasa since they did not accept the legitimacy of either of these actions.[12]

Despite the Nationalist government's recognition, the Panchen Lama decided to throw in his lot with the Chinese Communists since they seemed more likely to be able to help him return to Tibet. Thus, as soon as the People's Liberation "liberated" Qinghai province in September 1949, the Panchen Lama's officials made cordial contacts with them, and on October 1, 1949—the inauguration day of the new People's Republic of China—the Panchen Lama sent Mao Zedong the following telegram:

> For generations the Panchen has been treated most generously and bestowed many honours by the country [China]. For more than twenty years, I have never slackened my efforts to defend

the territorial integrity of Tibet, but nothing has been achieved, for which I feel most guilty. I am now staying in Qinghai, waiting for the order to return to Tibet. Thanks to the leadership of Your Excellencies, Northwest China has been liberated and the Central People's Government has been established—events that all the people who are proud of the country find highly inspiring. These accomplishments will surely bring happiness to the people and make it possible for the nation to stand on its feet again; and with these accomplishments the liberation of Tibet is only a matter of time. On behalf of all the Tibetan people, I pay Your Excellencies the highest respects and pledge our wholehearted support.[13]

The following year, Mao Zedong accepted that boy as the tenth Panchen Lama and agreed to restore his position in Tibet when it was reunified.[14]

Nevertheless, for most Tibetans, this Panchen Lama's legitimacy was in question since the Dalai Lama had not accepted him as the true reincarnation. Consequently, when the Dalai Lama's delegation arrived in Beijing in 1951 to negotiate the Seventeen-Point Agreement, China took steps to rectify this by insisting that the Tibetan side recognize the boy before the talks could begin. The Tibetan delegation had no religious authority to make such a judgment and was forced to telegraph the Dalai Lama for instructions. The Dalai Lama quickly performed a holy divination that conveniently confirmed the Qinghai boy as the true tenth Panchen Lama, and there the matter ended until his death in 1989.

Thus, despite the contested nature of the confirmation process, there was a recent precedent in which the Tashilhunpo monks and officials independently identified a candidate, the Chinese government accepted the boy without resort to a golden urn lottery, and the Dalai Lama subsequently confirmed the choice. However, despite this precedent, the confirmation of the new Panchen Lama ended in a political debacle.

Since Chadrel had already obtained the Dalai Lama's confirmation of Gendun Choekyi Nyima, it was absolutely essential that he secure China's approval of the boy. His plan apparently was that Beijing would first formally confirm the boy and then the Dalai Lama would indicate that he accepted the choice as correct. In other words, the previous precedent would be followed. Chinese media indicated that on about February 11, 1995, Chadrel Rimpoche sought to persuade the central government to dispense with the golden urn lottery, assuring them that this was in accordance with Tibetan customs and that his own divine lottery conducted before the stupa (religious tomb) of the late Panchen Lama in Tashilhunpo had determined that Gendun Choekyi Nyima was incontrovertibly the correct incarnation.[15] His efforts, apparently, were unsuccessful because Chinese sources indicate that in March 1995 the government asked Chadrel to submit three to five names for the golden urn drawing.[16] By the middle of the following month, reports indicated that Han and Tibetan officials in China were preparing to assemble for the installation ceremony, although nothing yet had been publicly announced. It was at this juncture that the Dalai Lama suddenly announced to the world on May 14, 1995, that he recognized Gendun Choekyi Nyima as the new Panchen Lama. His statement asserted that the Chinese government had no authority over this selection by saying, "The search and recognition of Panchen Rimpoche's reincarnation is a religious matter and not political."[17]

The announcement, of course, embarrassed and infuriated the Chinese government. Beijing had tried to do things in a "Tibetan" way through Chadrel Rimpoche and Tashilhunpo monastery, and had even approached the Dalai Lama to help, but now had been humiliatingly upstaged and made to seem irrelevant to the decision-making process. The Dalai Lama had shown the world that from exile he could decide the results of an incarnation search conducted within Tibet under the auspices of the Chinese government.

Why the Dalai Lama chose to do this, however, is unclear, and neither side has indicated what really happened. The official

Chinese version asserts that Chadrel illegally leaked (unspecified) state secrets to the Dalai Lama—Chadrel was sentenced to six years in prison in May 1997 for conspiring to split the nation and for betraying state secrets.[18] But were his contacts with the Dalai Lama really unsanctioned?

Chadrel clearly had state permission to meet Gyalo Thondup in Beijing and send a letter to the Dalai Lama through him, and the Dalai Lama's response, as mentioned earlier, was also "official" in that it was transmitted through the Chinese embassy in New Delhi. Moreover, Chadrel Rimpoche was a patriotic, pro-government lama whose political career had been based on opposing splittism and supporting Tibet as part of China. He was well known in government circles and trusted by the Tibet Autonomous Region Government (whom Beijing had placed in charge of the search). Consequently, it is unlikely that he decided on his own to interact secretly with the Dalai Lama on a matter of such obvious national importance. On the other hand, it is possible that while top officials in Beijing knew in general about the contacts, it did not know the details, particularly that Chadrel was sending information on all the candidates.

Whichever of the above scenarios is correct, it appears that when Chadrel tried to persuade the central government to dispense with the golden urn lottery, an impasse developed over whether eliminating the golden urn lottery might inadvertently allow the Dalai Lama to claim he had confirmed the candidate before Beijing, and if so, what should be done about this. While the issue was being debated in Beijing, Chadrel—this time certainly without informing anyone in the government—apparently contacted the Dalai Lama and conveyed to him news of the impasse. This information appears to have set in motion discussions in Dharamsala that ended with the Dalai Lama's preemptive announcement.[19]

Hopefully, the full details of this incident will be revealed in the coming years, but for the moment, what is important is its impact on the Tibet Question. Regardless of what transpired in China and India, the Dalai Lama's decision to preemptively announce the new Panchen Lama was, to say the least, politically inastute. Even if Beijing ultimately decided to select a different child, the Dalai Lama would have been able to denounce the choice and then specify his own selection. Alternatively, had Beijing ultimately decided to select the right boy, the Dalai Lama could have then given his critical seal of approval, confirming that the correct Panchen Lama was chosen. Both sides could then have claimed to their followers and the world their representation of what the event "really" meant, but the Dalai Lama would have sent a powerful political signal to Beijing's top leaders that he was genuinely interested in working with them to reduce conflict and overcome problems.

Since the Dalai Lama obviously knew his preemptory announcement would infuriate the Chinese, we must assume that either he actually wanted to show Beijing and the world his paramount role in this issue regardless of the political fallout, or he believed that his unilateral action was necessary to push China to choose the correct boy, the logic being that China would not reject his selection since it was also the choice of Chadrel Rimpoche (and thus Tashilhunpo monastery's own search team).

Whatever the Dalai Lama's motivation, his announcement was seen in China as a hostile political act aimed at embarrassing China and an example of the Dalai Lama's relentless pursuit of political kudos in the West at China's expense. From China's perspective, once again, at a critical time, the Dalai Lama had thumbed his nose at Beijing, sending a clear signal that when it got down to fishing or cutting bait, he still preferred cutting bait!

The Dalai Lama's announcement, of course, placed China in a difficult predicament. Since a basic prerequisite of the entire process was to affirm the Chinese central government's authority to select incarnations, Beijing had to decide whether it should challenge the Dalai Lama's (and, of course, its own search committee's) choice. If it agreed to the Dalai Lama's choice, it could give the appearance that it was merely following his more fundamental authority. However, if it did not and selected someone else, it might have a Panchen Lama that many (if not most) Tibetans refused to accept as genuine.

It took Beijing five months to come to a decision, but finally it disqualified Gendun Choekyi Nyima and used the golden urn lottery to select a different boy, whom the Chinese government formally confirmed in November 1995. The Dalai Lama and his supporters vociferously attacked this decision, portraying the boy as a false incarnation and charging Beijing with blatant infringement of Tibet's religious freedom and the Dalai Lama's historic prerogative. Beijing was placed on the defensive on this issue and still is. It now has a prominent incarnate lama whom most Tibetans are loathe to accept, and another boy, Gendun Choekyi Nyima, who must be kept under constant surveillance to prevent his being whisked off into exile—an act that would substantially compound the current debacle.

While many in exile and in the West see this as a victory for the Dalai Lama, it is hard to understand their logic. To be sure, it made Tibetans and their Western supporters feel good to see the Dalai Lama exert his authority over this issue, but the price he paid was substantial and the gains were minuscule. In practical terms, the Panchen Lama he selected is not safe in exile under his tutelage, so he has in effect relegated the boy he chose to a life of house arrest. This creates a powerful human rights issue for the exiles, but only at the cost of further fueling the distrust and animosity that many in China already feel toward him, just at the time when he is under increasing pressure to persuade China to soften its policies in Tibet. Moreover, his announcement has badly undermined the credibility of the more moderate Chinese officials who sold the State Council on the idea that an ethnically sensitive selection process would be in China's best interests. It has therefore reinforced the hard-liners' contention that China cannot trust or work with the Dalai Lama and set back chances that China will agree to renew talks with him. And it has allowed the "prize"—the new Panchen Lama—to fall under the control of China. If the Dalai Lama really wanted to play political hardball, it would have made more sense for him to select a Panchen Lama in exile to be educated and groomed as he saw fit.

But such is the nature of the Tibet Question. Even when both sides have a common interest in preventing a disaster, emotion and issues of "face"—political pride—easily derail them and marginalize reason. The Dalai Lama knows intellectually that he needs more friends and supporters in Beijing, not Washington or New York City, but he finds it emotionally difficult to take appropriate actions to achieve that end.

In the wake of the Panchen Lama debacle, Beijing has intensified its propaganda attacks on the Dalai Lama, using a new level of crude and insulting language. This anti–Dalai Lama campaign has continued to the present, and many in China are convinced that waiting until the sixty-two-year-old Dalai Lama dies is the simplest answer to their "Tibet" problem. At the same time, the Chinese government is proceeding full speed with its policy of developing and modernizing Tibet. It hopes this policy will solidify its position in Tibet regardless of what the Dalai Lama or Tibetans think or do, and will ultimately create a new generation of Tibetans who consider it in their interests to be a part of China. If nothing else, this policy will so radically change the demographic composition of Tibet and the nature of its economy, that failure to win over a new generation of Tibetans will not weaken Beijing's control over Tibet.

Consequently, from the Chinese side, conditions now are not highly conducive to serious participation in a negotiated solution, let alone dramatic concessions. Beijing's integrationist policy is progressing, its trust of the Dalai Lama is at an all-time low, and the absence of a credible threat of external sanctions from the United States, Europe, and Japan allows them to pursue this with impunity.

On the other hand, the death of Deng Xiaoping in February of 1997 has provided the Dalai Lama a tiny new window of opportunity. It is clear that many experts and moderates in China disagree with the assumptions underlying the current hard-line approach and question whether the current policy will produce the long-term stability in Tibet that China wants. They realize that it is exacerbating the alienation of Tibetans, even young ones, intensifying their feelings of ethnic hatred and political hopelessness, and inculcating the idea that Tibetans cannot have their nationalistic aspirations met as part of the People's Republic of China. Some latent sentiment remains, therefore, that the long-term interests of China would be best served by returning to a more ethnically sensitive Tibet policy. Consequently, if a new, stable leadership emerges in Beijing, it might be interested in reviving talks should the proper signals be received from the Dalai Lama. Settling the Tibet Question would certainly represent a historic victory for any Chinese leader. It is, therefore, not too late for a breakthrough, but the Dalai Lama will have to make the first move. Right now the hard-liners on Tibet are in control, and they will remain so unless something gives the more moderate elements in Beijing and Lhasa new leverage. That new leverage can only be provided by the Dalai Lama.

THE DALAI LAMA AND DHARAMSALA

The situation in the exile community is not favorable to the kinds of major concessions by which the Dalai Lama could resolve the current impasse. To be sure, he and his top officials are desperately anxious to stop the influx of non-Tibetans into Tibet since they are convinced that their culture, religion, and language cannot flourish if Tibet is swamped, even with only a "floating" population. They hold deep nationalistic convictions

that a Tibetan homeland should be preserved, whether independent from or part of China; consequently they are encouraging supporters in the West to urge Beijing to resume talks
with them and have approached other countries to intercede
on their behalf. The Dalai Lama has also taken new initiatives,
recently writing Party General Secretary Jiang Zemin to indicate that he would like to make a religious visit to China—
specifically a "nonpolitical" pilgrimage to a Buddhist holy site
in Shanxi province called Wutaishan. And, in a condolence letter sent to Jiang Zemin when Deng Xiaoping died (in February
1997), the Dalai Lama said,

> It is very regrettable that serious negotiations on the issue of
> Tibet could not take place during Mr. Deng's lifetime. However,
> I firmly believe that the absence of Mr. Deng provides new op-
> portunities and challenges for both Tibetans and the Chinese. I
> very much hope that under your leadership the government of
> China will realize the wisdom of resolving the issue of Tibet
> through negotiations in a spirit of reconciliation and compro-
> mise. For my part I remain committed to the belief that our
> problem can be solved only through negotiations, held in an at-
> mosphere of sincerity and openness.[20]

Furthermore, at the time of his 1997 trip to Taiwan, the Dalai
Lama went out of his way to indicate that he is willing to accept Tibet as a part of China:

> "My [proposed] trip to Taiwan clearly proves that I have aban-
> doned the position of Tibet independence," the Dalai Lama was
> quoted as saying in an interview with the *United Daily News*. . .
>   "Because Taiwan recognizes Tibet as part of China, my visit
> to Taiwan indicates my agreement with that position. I am not
> asking for Tibet independence. This point is also very obvious,"
> the Dalai Lama told the newspaper from his office in India.[21]

China has not agreed to a visit by the Dalai Lama, even one
disguised as a religious pilgrimage. A lot of water has gone
under the bridge since 1989 when Beijing itself asked the Dalai
Lama to visit on a religious mission. The Chinese leadership

does not believe that a new round of talks would be fruitful because the Dalai Lama continues to insist on political autonomy for Tibet similar to the plan advanced in the Strasbourg address. For example, the Reuters News Agency reported that during a recent trip to Taiwan "The Dalai Lama said that despite some Tibetan opposition, he favoured for his homeland the 'one country, two systems' formula of wide local autonomy under China's sovereignty that Beijing will be pioneering in Hong Kong this year and hopes to spread to Taiwan. 'I believe very much in the spirit of one country, two systems,' the 61-year-old monk told a news briefing, repeating that he sought only self-rule for Tibet, not independence."[22]

Thus, the question facing the Dalai Lama (and his leaders) now is similar to the one they confronted in 1982 when their first delegation went to Beijing—how much less than independence are they willing to accept? Is political self-rule the absolute minimum or should further concessions be accepted? Is time on the Dalai Lama's side or is it running out? And if it is running out, is this the year to make a move, or might next year not be better? The fundamental impasse is the same as it was in the early 1980s—China appears categorically unwilling to give Tibet the right to a different political system—self-rule—and the Dalai Lama is unwilling to accept less than that. What is new, however, is China's current hard-line policy, which is exerting tremendous pressure on the Dalai Lama and his leaders either to quickly resolve the conflict or to develop effective countermeasures that will prevent China from changing the ethnic and economic character of Tibet.

The Dalai Lama has several options. He can continue his current international campaign, trying to keep China on the defensive in the global arena through human rights attacks while striving to garner more support for his cause in Washington and Europe. The Dalai Lama and his supporters have become extraordinarily adept at this. However, the reality of the situation is that the United States and other Western countries have clearly demonstrated they are unwilling to alienate China over human rights in general or Tibet in particular. Thus, like players on a losing football team who are awarded stars for their helmets for good plays, these international successes make everyone feel good but do not change the outcome of the contest. And to the extent that they antagonize the Chinese and encourage rigidity among the exile leadership, they may exacerbate an already dangerous situation.

Implicit in continuing the current policy is hope—the exiles' hope that the flow of history itself will provide the victory they desire, that Communist China will soon disintegrate like the Qing dynasty in 1911 and the USSR in 1991, and that this will afford them the opportunity to regain control over Tibet. The Tibetan folk saying "Tibetan hopeful, Chinese suspicious" has a special resonance in the current political atmosphere in Dharamsala. For the Dalai Lama the current approach is primarily a waiting strategy—while waiting for history to solve his dilemma in a satisfactory manner, the Dalai Lama is trying to keep the Tibet Question alive internationally. This is the safe option for Dharamsala and the Dalai Lama.

However, there is an obvious disadvantage to this course of action—or inaction. Tibet is being transformed in a manner the exile leadership abhors, and if the current process continues for any length of time, this transformation will likely be difficult to reverse. Time appears not to be on the Dalai Lama's side. Moreover, the death of Deng Xiaoping in 1997 ushered in a new chapter of Chinese history. Deng supported the hardline shift away from Hu Yaobang's policy, so his death is seen in Dharamsala as removing an important impediment to Beijing's potential flexibility. Consequently, there is increasing pressure on Dharamsala to persuade China to deal with the Dalai Lama by moving in one of two directions.

One direction would be serious compromise—the Dalai Lama could send Beijing clear and dramatic signals that he is ready to engage in realistic talks, i.e., to accept less than true political autonomy. This would be somewhat analogous to President Nixon and National Security Advisor Kissinger signalling Washington's serious wish to normalize Sino-American relations by unilaterally relaxing bans on American contact and trade with China, by moving the U.S. 7th Fleet out of the Taiwan Straits, and by starting to talk about the "People's Republic of China" instead of using more derogatory terms like "Red China" or "Chinese Communists." Taking such a step, however, would be excruciatingly difficult for the Dalai Lama since it would likely split the fragile unity of the exile community.[23] In a sense, therefore, it would mean placing the interests of the 4 million Tibetans in Tibet ahead of the interests of the 130,000 Tibetans in exile, and would require the Dalai Lama to eschew more empty but emotionally satisfying "stars" for his helmet. This will be very difficult for him to do without the strong conviction that his compromise initiative will be successful.

An alternative strategic option would be escalation—encouraging (or organizing) violent opposition in Tibet as a means of exerting new leverage for concessions from China. Throughout the 1980s both sides have adjusted their tactics to counter their opponent's initiatives; a campaign of terroristic violence would conform to this pattern by preventing China from pursuing business as usual in Tibet. Such a strategy would seek not to drive China out of Tibet but rather to persuade Beijing that unless it adopted a more conciliatory line toward the Dalai Lama, Tibetans would disrupt life in Tibet and other parts of China. Very likely such a strategy would be based outside of Tibet and carried out by small units of trained and dedicated militants, but it could well spread within Tibet.

If such a strategy of violence were successful, it could help to destabilize China during the dangerous period of leadership transition. But if even only partially successful, it could curtail tourism in Tibet, impede the growth of overseas investment there, threaten the security of all non-Tibetans in Tibet, and heighten international awareness of the seriousness of the problem. It would, in essence, seek to demonstrate to China the futility of the hard-line policy by showing that the ethnic sensibilities of Tibetans cannot be discounted. If done effectively, such attacks would be impossible for China to prevent without again resorting to martial law in Tibet, but even then, Tibetan militants could easily respond by shifting their attention from Tibet to Tibet-related targets in Sichuan, Qinghai, and Beijing. Without changing its entire open-door policy for tourists and businesspeople, Beijing could not prevent explosives from entering its major points of entry in Eastern China.

However, like the compromise option, this resort to force would be extremely difficult for the Dalai Lama to sanction given his strong feelings about nonviolence, but it may also be difficult for him to prevent.[24] His own failure to force China to moderate its policies at a time when the character of Tibet is so obviously being altered could lead more militant Tibetans to declare his civil disobedience approach a failure and turn to more violent approaches on their own. The crux of the matter is that Tibetans are unlikely to stand indefinitely on the sidelines watching Beijing transform their homeland with impunity. Nationalistic emotions coupled with desperation and anger make a powerful brew, and there are Tibetans inside and outside of Tibet who are intoxicated with the idea of beginning such a campaign of focused violence—in their view a "war of conscience," a Tibetan-style *intifada*.

Even now it appears that Tibetans in exile are seeking outside funding to organize and launch such activities. The real question, therefore, may not be *will* they, but *when* will they decide they can wait no longer to do so. Already in 1996 three bombings occurred in Lhasa, the last a large blast that damaged a government office building and neighboring hotels, and shook houses up to half a mile away.[25] Although these attacks targeted buildings not innocent civilians, the specter of Tibet engulfed in the kind of ethnic violence found in the Middle East and Northern Ireland is not all that far-fetched given the current frustration and anger Tibetans feel and their strategic need to create powerful new leverage with Beijing.

Consequently, the Tibet Question appears to have reached a critical juncture in its long history. Both sides seem incapable of taking the risks necessary to work out a compromise solution to the conflict, preferring instead to continue developing adversarial strategies and tactics designed to thwart their opponent and register gains for their own side. However, as the exiles become more and more impotent to change the situation in Tibet, their frustration will increase and the danger of serious violence will increase exponentially, with or without the Dalai Lama's approval.

THE UNITED STATES AND
THE TIBET QUESTION

This book is not the appropriate venue to detail the tacks and turns of U.S.–Tibet relations over the past five decades;[26] it suffices to reiterate that U.S. support for Tibet diminished substantially after Nixon and Kissinger initiated rapprochement with China in 1969–1971.[27] For the decade following détente, Tibet remained an obscure issue in U.S. foreign policy. The Dalai Lama was not even permitted to visit the United States until 1979. Events in the 1980s, however, brought the Tibet Question to the forefront again. The Dalai Lama's international initiative garnered strong sympathy and support for Tibet in Congress, in the human rights community, and among citizens' lobbying groups, and was able to move the Tibet issue from the rarefied atmosphere of professional "foreign affairs" to the more visceral arena of domestic U.S. politics.[28]

Congress took the lead, initiating a variety of measures in support of the Dalai Lama such as the 1987 pro-Tibet legislation mentioned in the previous chapter, the 1987 invitation to address the Congressional Human Rights Caucus, the authorization of Tibetan language broadcasts on the Voice of America (in 1990), the creation of a Fulbright scholarship program for Tibetans in India and Nepal, the legislation mandating that the State Department's "Country Reports on Human Rights" include a section on Tibet *separate* from China, and legislation mandating that the State Department issue a report "on the state of relations between the United States and those recognized by Congress *as the true representatives of the Tibetan people; the Dalai Lama, his representatives, and the Tibetan Government in exile,* and on conditions in Tibet" (italics added).[29] Congress also created Radio Free Asia (with a Tibet language broadcast section), and in 1996 included a proviso in the State Department Authorization Act calling for a "special envoy for Tibet" with ambassadorial status. The special envoy's proposed function was to encourage negotiations between the Dalai Lama's representatives and China, coordinate the administration's response to congressional concerns about Tibet, travel to Tibet and the Tibetan settlements in exile, and promote good relations between the Tibetan government in exile and the U.S. government.[30] Although this last initiative failed when President Clinton vetoed the entire State Department appropriations bill, the "envoy" idea will likely be raised again as the pro-Tibet lobby in Congress tries to nudge U.S. official policy closer to accepting Tibet as an entity separate from China.

The United States has also experienced an explosion of popular attention and support for the Dalai Lama and his cause, including the organization of Tibet lobbying groups throughout the United States (and much of the Western world), the increasing attention of human rights organizations on civil liberties in Tibet, and the involvement of entertainment glitterati such as Harrison Ford, Richard Gere, Philip Glass, and the late Allen Ginsberg. The Dalai Lama himself has in some senses become a pop-culture icon.

The broad popular and congressional interest in Tibet has pressured recent administrations to take more cognizance of the Dalai Lama and Tibet than they might otherwise have done. President Bush, for example, not only met with the Dalai Lama in private,[31] but in 1991 signed a State Department Authorization Act that included a number of very strong (albeit nonbinding) statements on Tibet such as the following:

> It is the sense of the Congress that—
>
> (1) Tibet, including those areas incorporated into the Chinese provinces of Sichuan, Yunnan, Gansu, and Qinghai, is *an occupied country* under established principles of international law
>
> (2) Tibet's true representatives are the Dalai Lama and the Tibetan Government in Exile as recognized by the Tibetan people. [emphasis added][32]

The inauguration of Bill Clinton in 1993 saw further escalation of presidential involvement. As part of a new China policy in which higher priority was to be given to issues of human rights and democracy in foreign affairs, Clinton openly criticized China's actions in Tibet. For example, when he announced on May 28, 1993, that the secretary of state would not recommend most favored nation (MFN) status for China in 1994 unless it made significant progress with respect to a series of human rights problems, he included the problem of "protecting Tibet's distinctive religious and cultural heritage." Six months later, when Mr. Clinton met Chinese Party General Secretary Jiang Zemin face-to-face in Seattle, he urged Jiang to improve cultural and religious freedom in Tibet and to open talks with the Dalai Lama.[33] The United States, for the first time, appeared willing to use its muscle to try to force changes in Chinese policy toward Tibet (although its position on the sovereignty issue had not changed). The year 1993 therefore seemed to many Tibetans and their supporters a major turning point in U.S.–Tibetan relations—if MFN was denied to China in part because of its policies in Tibet, the Tibetan exiles would have attained precisely the kind of leverage they had been seeking since the mid 1980s.

However, as we know, that did not come to pass. America's China policy reversed itself radically in 1994 when President Clinton announced he would not use economic sanctions to try to induce political changes in China, let alone Tibet.[34] Human rights was no longer linked to MFN, and the Tibetan exiles were thrust back virtually to square one. It was a painful disappointment.

In the three years since delinkage, the Clinton administration has given geopolitical and economic interests precedence over those of human rights and political freedom. Tibet has had a low profile in administration dealings with China, although some involved with U.S. foreign policy still contend that assisting Tibet is a matter of principle and conscience— that Tibet is an important test of U.S. will to take the lead in forging a new, more democratic, post–Cold War world. The majority viewpoint in the administration and State Department, however, disagrees, holding that the United States has no strategic interest in Tibet and that it should avoid letting the Tibet Question impair Sino-American relations. China is simply considered strategically too important. Terming its approach "comprehensive engagement," the Clinton administration argues that the best way to deal with China is not to attack and isolate it for its lack of civil rights and democracy, but rather to engage it in a positive sense. A 1994 State Department report on Tibet prepared for the Congress conveyed this rationale for engagement: "The ability of the United States to promote respect for human rights by the Chinese authorities is closely related to the strength of our bilateral relations with China. A serious disruption of U.S.–China relations would gravely undermine any hope for the United States to foster greater respect for the human rights of ethnic Tibetans in China."[35] Central to the Clinton administration's comprehensive engagement strategy is the desire to assure China that the United States does not challenge its claims to sovereignty over Tibet. The 1994 report conveyed this assurance through a very tough, anti-Dharamsala statement of the United States position on the political status of Tibet.

> Historically, the United States has acknowledged Chinese sovereignty over Tibet. Since at least 1966, U.S. policy has explicitly recognized the Tibetan Autonomous Region . . . as part of the People's Republic of China. This long-standing policy is consistent with the view of the entire international community, including all China's neighbors: no country recognizes Tibet as a sovereign state. Because we do not recognize Tibet as an independent state, the United States does not conduct diplomatic relations with the *self-styled* "Tibetan government-in-exile." [emphasis added][36]

Nevertheless, the Clinton administration finds it impossible to totally ignore human rights issues because of the powerful China and Tibet lobby, and it has had to walk a careful line between speaking up for religious and civil freedoms in China (and therefore in Tibet) and taking actions that would seriously disrupt Sino-American relations. In general it has tried to mollify domestic critics through carefully crafted gestures of sympathy and concern that carry minimal risk of impairing Sino-American relations—for example, meetings for the Dalai Lama in Washington with high officials such as the secretary of state and the vice-president (with presidential "drop-by" visits and photo ops), by not challenging the inflammatory language in the "sense of the Congress" provisions, and by making occasional statements urging China and Tibet to resolve the conflict peacefully. The Clinton administration has also felt compelled to continue criticizing China's human rights record, although not to the extent of applying sanctions. Just this year, for example, the United States again cosponsored a UN resolution (at the

UN Human Rights Commission in Geneva) that faulted China's human rights record. That draft resolution included language about Tibet, one clause expressing concern "at increased restrictions on the exercise of cultural, religious and other freedoms of Tibetans, including the case of the 11th Panchen Lama, Gendun Choekyi Nyima" and another clause calling upon the government of China "to preserve and protect the distinct cultural, ethnic, linguistic and religious identity of Tibetans."[37] However, as with previous resolutions, China had little trouble blocking this initiative, even preventing debate on the resolution. The absence of a Western democratic consensus on confronting China on issues of democracy and human rights is illustrated by the fact that France, Germany, Italy, Spain, Greece, Australia, and Canada declined to cosponsor Denmark's UN resolution,[38] and the United States appeared to be less than energetic in its support.

Consequently, when one looks back at the past decade of America's involvement in the Tibet Question, it appears clear that U.S. actions have not helped resolve the dispute or even moderated Chinese policies in Tibet. They have helped skyrocket the Dalai Lama's renown in the West and have made Tibetans both in exile and in Tibet feel good, but have not stopped the situation on the ground in Tibet from worsening (from the Dalai Lama's point of view). The jumble of lofty moralistic rhetoric and sympathetic gestures has not exerted meaningful pressure on China; nor, if the truth be told, was it meant to. Moreover, U.S. involvement has not been simply harmless—it has had serious negative consequences, for America's token actions have led many Tibetans to believe that it supports the Dalai Lama's wish for democracy in Tibet and encouraged them to continue opposing China. I remember vividly a twelve-year-old monk arguing with me about this once when I was doing research in Drepung monastery near Lhasa. He came up to me and asked, in a whisper, when the United States was going to push China out of Tibet and help the Dalai Lama return. When I tried to explain that China is a powerful country and the United States is not likely to do anything concrete, he refused to listen, saying emphatically, "No, no, I know the U.S. is more powerful than China and is going to help us."

Thus, the view of many in Beijing that the United States is "stirring up" Tibetans and threatening China's strategic interests in Tibet by trying to destabilize an important frontier region (as the CIA tried to do there in the 1950s and 1960s) is not without basis. This belief has helped to undercut the more conciliatory Chinese advocates of ethnically sensitive policies, who have been criticized within the Communist party for supporting a policy that is fostering riots and hatred in Tibet rather than greater friendship and acceptance of being part of China. United States policy, therefore, has inadvertently strengthened the hand of the very hard-liners in China whose policies the Dalai Lama seeks to reverse. Consequently, it is hard not to conclude that American expressions of support for Tibet and the Dalai Lama have been inherently counterproductive and the latest example of the Western "bad friend" syndrome. The U.S. government and the Congress make sympathetic but innocuous gestures of support, but carefully avoid using their might to induce China to compromise on terms the Dalai Lama is willing to accept; in the process they foster conditions that lead Beijing to consider a hard-line policy in Tibet to be in its national interests.

The Clinton administration's reluctance to become more actively involved in the Tibet Question makes *realpolitik* sense as long as the Sino-Tibetan conflict is unlikely to deteriorate into serious violence. However, as indicated above, increased anti-Chinese violence now seems distinctly probable. The ramifications of such an escalation would be substantial. If serious terroristic violence erupts in Tibet, it will inevitably be followed by a heavy-handed Chinese military response, which in turn will create powerful pressures in the U.S. domestic political arena for America to support what will be portrayed as the Tibetans' "struggle for freedom." Any such support would of course be perceived in Beijing as a direct and serious threat to China's core strategic interests and would substantially worsen the already fragile relations between China and the United States, potentially complicating America's entire Asia policy.

Serious violence in Tibet could also affect the internal stability of China itself. It might escalate and precipitate a chain of events that would destabilize China at this very important juncture in its history, or push the process of leadership transition toward the anti–U.S. hard-liners. One of Beijing's worst case scenarios is for serious disturbances in Tibet to spread to other minority areas such as Xinjiang and Inner Mongolia—or worse, to become coordinated with them. Given that the exiles and their supporters see Soviet-like disintegration in China as their hope of hopes, they are likely to leap in with alacrity at any sign of major economic or political instability during China's leadership change with the aim of exacerbating and accelerating this instability. All Tibetan leaders know the precedent of the thirteenth Dalai Lama's organizing military action in 1912 from exile in India and within a year expelling Manchu and Chinese officials and troops. United States policy toward Tibet therefore appears flawed since it is neither exerting pressure to bring about a peaceful resolution of the conflict nor preventing the exiles (and / or Tibetans in Tibet) from launching a strategy of violence.

Of course, it can be argued that Tibetans will not be able to organize and sustain a program of terrorist attacks against China—or will not have the stomach to do so—but it seems short-sighted for the United States to allow the situation to deteriorate to a state where this will be tested empirically. The current U.S. policy is allowing a dangerously volatile situation to develop according to its own momentum when its most likely outcome is clearly not in the strategic interests of the United States. At the very least, such a turn to violence could negatively affect Sino-American relations, and at the most, it might precipitate or exacerbate centrifugal forces in China that would foster political chaos in that key Asian nation.

But is there a reasonable compromise solution that could meet the needs of both parties to this conflict, and if so, what would it entail?

In order to achieve success, a compromise solution will have to satisfy the strategic and prestige needs of China while at the same time preserve a Tibetan homeland that is strongly Tibetan in language, culture, and demographic composition. Tibetans essentially desire a nationalistic settlement in which the political and the ethnic units are congruent. Tibet, according to this view, should be composed predominately of Tibetans, should be governed by Tibetans using their own language, and should allow the free expression of Tibetan culture and religion. For Dharamsala, the optimum venue is independence or complete political autonomy (something like the Strasbourg proposal or the "one country, two systems" approach being used for Hong Kong). However, as we have seen, these options are unacceptable to China and therefore do not represent a realistic common ground for creating a resolution of the problem. If Hu Yaobang could not accept a such federation status for Tibet, it is unrealistic to expect Deng Xiaoping's successors to do so. The Dalai Lama will have to lower his bottom line to foster a compromise solution.

Throughout this century, Tibet's search for an acceptable political niche in relation to its large and powerful neighbor has been ineffectual, and the current disparity in wealth and power makes its position weaker than ever before.[39] Tibetans may feel it is not fair to expect them to compromise on principle just because of the might of their opponent, and it is difficult not to sympathize with this view, but history has dealt them a very poor hand and events in Tibet appear to be altering the situation at a rapid pace. If they do nothing now but chalk up more and more symbolic victories—more shiny stars for their already star-filled helmets—in a few decades when the Dalai Lama dies (he is now sixty-two), there may no longer be a distinctive Tibetan homeland.

The key question regarding a compromise resolution, therefore, is whether it is possible to create a truly "ethnic" Tibet within the framework Beijing is willing to accept—that is, without changing the underlying Communist political system. I think the answer is yes, if both sides agree to a number of important concessions and work to set aside past hatred and distrust.

China, for its part, would have to make major concessions, restoring Tibet as a linguistically and demographically homogeneous territory. This could be a risky step for Beijing, but could be rationalized domestically because Tibet was incorporated into the People's Republic of China through a unique written covenant, the Seventeen-Point Agreement.

In the political sphere, a "new" Tibet Autonomous Region would retain its current political system, but Beijing would move in stages to appoint Tibetans to head all its party and government offices, including the position of first secretary of the party. By the end of a ten-year phase-in period, the percentage of Tibetan officials would increase substantially from its current 60–70 percent to as high as 85–90 percent.

In the cultural sphere, a variety of measures would have to be implemented to enhance the degree to which Tibetan culture predominates. One of the most critical of these would be to phase in Tibetan as the basic operating language of government. Although all Tibetan offices and higher officials would have to be bilingual in Chinese, and the education system would continue to teach Chinese along with Tibetan, restoring written Tibetan as the language of the government of Tibet would enable Tibetan culture to grow and modernize to a degree not now possible. A detailed plan for this reform was developed in 1987–1988 at the urging of the Panchen Lama and Ngabö, and it could readily be activated. Other cultural measures such as eliminating restrictions on the number of monks in monasteries and permitting Buddhist clerics from abroad to give religious instruction, could be worked out by the parties and gradually phased in.

In the critical demographic and economic spheres Beijing would have to take measures that would substantially decrease the number of non-Tibetans living in Tibet and reduce outside economic competition (from other provinces) so that Tibetans become the main beneficiaries of economic development in the TAR. Beijing's emphasis on economic development would continue since Tibetans want economic progress, but if need be at a slightly slower rate since the prime consideration would be their direct economic welfare. Because the overwhelming majority of non-Tibetans in Tibet are not legal residents (colonists), Beijing has no responsibility for their resettlement and reemployment, and could send them home, although this would be a sensitive issue. A reasonable goal would be a gradual return to the demographic situation present at the time of the Tibetan uprising of 1959 when rural and urban Tibet were overwhelmingly Tibetan in population and character.

The result of such a process would be a Tibet that was predominately Tibetan in culture, language, and demographic composition. It would continue to modernize but would be run by Tibetans, albeit "Communist" Tibetans. This kind of Tibet would probably meet with the approval of the overwhelming majority of Tibetans in Tibet (if they felt external support was not forthcoming for something more). If China in time follows the path of Taiwan and evolves more democratic institutions such as multiple political parties, the political leadership in Tibet would similarly broaden its base. The underlying premise of this compromise solution is that transforming Tibet into a modern society is perfectly compatible with preserving its rich language, culture, and religion, and that it is in the interests of both sides to facilitate such a development.

Political freedom in the Western sense is secondary to preserving ethnic, demographic, and cultural homogeneity.

One of the greatest stumbling blocks to such a solution is the exiles' demand for a Greater Tibet. Amdo and Kham, to be sure, are ecologically, culturally, and religiously similar to political Tibet, but historical differences and current political realities make the creation of a Greater Tibet extremely improbable, at least initially. A possible solution to this impasse would be for Beijing to implement parallel changes in the Tibet Autonomous Region and in ethnographic Tibet, and for both sides to agree to delay addressing the unification issue until the new program has been in operation for five or ten years and new relations of trust, confidence, and respect are established.

Beijing now considers, with considerable justification, that even a "cultural-ethnic" solution such as this would be a potential threat to its position in Tibet given the strong anti-Chinese and proseparatist feelings of Tibetans and the equivocal attitude of the Dalai Lama. Consequently, to receive favorable consideration in China, such a compromise plan would have to include components that clearly reinforced Beijing's sovereignty over Tibet and enhanced its long-term political control there.

Only the Dalai Lama can provide this for Beijing, so he, rather than the exile government, is the key element in such a compromise. Beijing, in fact, assiduously refuses to recognize the Dharamsala government in exile, insisting it is dealing only with the Dalai Lama about his return. To win the concessions outlined here, the Dalai Lama would have to agree to do several things. First he would have to return to China/Tibet and publicly accept Chinese sovereignty over Tibet. Second he would have to work actively to create cooperative and harmonious relations between Tibetans and non-Tibetans, persuading Tibetans in Lhasa to stop disturbances and accept that a truly Tibetan Tibet is not incompatible with being a part of

China. He would have to use his enormous prestige and charisma to change the attitude of Tibetans (in Tibet) toward being part of China. His stature in Tibet is so great that he could certainly do that if he tried and if Beijing supported his efforts by promptly phasing in the changes suggested here.[40] Once begun, such a process could be implemented over a decade, even if most Tibetans in exile chose not to return. For China, this solution would close the book on the Tibet Question since major support for Tibetan independence in the West would end if the Dalai Lama accepted such a solution. For the Dalai Lama, it would mean preserving a true, homogeneous ethnic homeland for his people.

However, this kind of compromise is unlikely to occur without external assistance. Because there is no consensus in the exile community about the advantages of such a cultural compromise, let alone about the exclusion of ethnographic Tibet, the Dalai Lama would very likely have to pursue this course of action on his own—without the unified support of his government in exile. And he would have to launch it by unilaterally sending Beijing unambiguous signals that he was finally willing to work with them (on the cultural level) to settle the Tibet Question. It would not be an easy decision, and as in the past, his tendency will be to resist this. A key to working out such an agreement will be the development of new relations of trust and respect between the leaders of China and the Dalai Lama. However, as the debacle over the selection of the new Panchen Lama illustrated, it is easier to revert to old confrontational patterns than to forge new conciliatory ones.

Consequently, if China and the Dalai Lama are left to their own devices, a negotiated resolution of the conflict along these lines is unlikely at present. The parties involved have simply too little trust and too many powerful reasons for not taking a risk. If progress is to be made, therefore, a "catalyst-facilitator" is needed, and this is where the United States could play a constructive role, either directly through private diplomacy, or through a proxy country such as Norway (or Mongolia). It would be injudicious to spell out publicly how this U.S. participation might occur, but suffice it to say that given the low level of trust of China among Tibetans, the Dalai Lama will need strong encouragement before he can send the kind of bold signal that could catch Beijing's attention. In particular, he will need reassurances that should China renege on its commitments once he returned to China, the United States would take strong action to protect him. On the other hand, the United States would also want to make private assurances to Beijing that it will support the new arrangement vociferously, regardless of diehard critics in Congress or the West.

Moving in this direction would entail some risk for the United States given China's extreme sensitivity to outside intervention in its internal affairs, and because congressional critics might well accuse the administration of selling out the Dalai Lama to the Communists, but if done discreetly, and with the agreement of the Dalai Lama, these risks can be minimized. In any case, the potential benefit to U.S. national interests far outweighs the political risks. Not only would it prevent the Tibet Question from negatively influencing Sino-American relations, it would accord with U.S humanitarian principles by helping Tibetans preserve Tibet as a true cultural and ethnic homeland. It would therefore make America the first important Western democracy to move beyond the "bad friend" syndrome.

The Tibet Question has currently reached a dangerous turning point. The Chinese are pursuing a policy that the Dalai Lama knows is changing Tibet, perhaps irretrievably, and that the situation will only worsen in time. Although the dominant view in Beijing is that this policy serves the long-term interests of the People's Republic of China, it is obvious to many in China that a policy that creates anger, enmity, demonstrations, and violence among Tibetans is not really ensuring the long-term security and goodwill China wants. If Tibetans and Chinese are ever to reach a secure and meaningful rapprochement, Tibetans' deep-seated ethnic sensitivities must, at the very least, be addressed. The death of Deng Xiaoping offers a uniquely appropriate opportunity to make a new effort to resolve the problem.

The Dalai Lama is central to such a compromise resolution. At sixty-two, he must be thinking about how best to preserve his people and their way of life in his remaining years. His predecessor, the thirteenth Dalai Lama, made a disastrous decision in the 1920s when, under pressure from conservatives, he dismantled the officer corps and the core of the modernization program. The fourteenth Dalai Lama now stands at another crossroads, contemplating how to preserve a "Tibetan" Tibet for future generations of his people. He may continue to sit on the sidelines, hoping that external forces will destroy his enemy, but it is more likely that he will soon feel compelled to adopt a proactive approach—either moving to preserve Tibet by accepting a major compromise like the one outlined here, or by tacitly and reluctantly accepting a new tactic of countering Chinese policies in Tibet through organized violence. It seems clearly in the interests of the United States and sympathetic Americans to develop a strategy that will ensure that the Dalai Lama and his leaders choose the former over the latter.

Notes

PREFACE

1. Moynihan 1994, pp. 66, 150.
2. The U.S. example, of course, illustrates the issue of self-determination, not nationalism.
3. Rong and Naigu 1994, p. 509.
4. Richardson 1984, pp. 1–2.
5. Victory in the representational war can be important. Despite the historical reality, the Tibetan exile government's representation of the invasion has generally prevailed—the U.S. Congress, for example, consistently refers to the invasion of Tibet as occurring in 1949 rather than 1950.

THE IMPERIAL ERA

1. Shakabpa 1967, pp. 39–40.
2. These events were recorded in inscriptions carved on stone pillars in Lhasa that still exist. See Richardson 1985 for text of the treaty of 821/822 A.D.
3. Kolmas 1967, pp. 12–15.
4. Shakabpa 1967, p. 63.
5. Ibid.; Rossabi 1988, p. 41.
6. Personal communication, E. Sperling, April, 1997.
7. Shakabpa 1967, p. 133.
8. Ya 1991, pp. 47–48.
9. De Filippi 1937, p. 170.
10. Ya 1991, p. 52.

11. Kolmas 1967, pp. 41–42. Some of these areas such as Litang and Batang were returned to Tibetan jurisdiction in 1735.

12. Communication from the Qing emperor Gaozong to the new *amban* after the death of Pholhanas, cited in Ya 1991, p. 55.

13. Dung dkar 1983, pp. 124–125.

14. The names and dates of birth of each candidate were to be written in the Manchu, Han, and Tibetan lanuages on metal slips and placed in a golden urn provided by the Manchu emperor. After prayers before the statue of the Buddha in the Jokhang temple in Lhasa, a slip was drawn, the Buddha ensuring that the correct slip was selected.

15. This document was jointly drafted by Fu Kang'an, the incarnate lama Kyirong Hutuktu (representing the Dalai Lama), and the head administrator of the Panchen Lama. A translation appears in Ya 1991, pp. 72–83.

16. Ya 1991, p. 72.

17. Ibid., pp. 83–84.

18. Phuntso Tashi 1995, p. 296.

19. Lamb 1960, p. 146.

20. Richardson 1984, p. 78.

21. Ibid., p. 91.

22. Ibid., p. 272.

23. Ibid., p. 274. For more details on this period see: Goldstein 1989; Lamb 1966; Richardson 1984; Snellgrove and Richardson 1980; Ya 1991.

24. Teichman 1922, p. 14.

25. Goldstein 1989, p. 51.

26. Ibid., pp. 51–52.

INTERLUDE: DE FACTO
INDEPENDENCE

1. Teichman 1922, p. 18.

2. Goldstein 1989, pp. 59–60.

3. Grasso, Corrin, and Kort 1991, p. 72.

4. Li 1960, p. 130.

5. Goldstein 1989, pp. 68–70.

6. Ibid., pp. 71–73.

7. See Lamb 1989, pp. 13–14, for a cogent discussion of Simla.

8. See Goldstein 1989, pp. 41–212, for a detailed examination of this period.

CHINESE COMMUNIST RULE:
THE MAO ERA

1. Goldstein 1989, p. 392 (cited from *U.S. Foreign Relations, 1942,* 103.91802/687).

2. Woodrow Wilson's lofty commitment to freedom and self-determination can be seen from his February 11, 1918, speech to a joint session of Congress when he stated that, "National aspirations must be respected; peoples may now be dominated and governed only by their own consent. 'Self-determination' is not a mere phrase. It is an imperative principle of action which statesmen will henceforth ignore at their peril" (cited in Moynihan 1994, pp. 78–79).

3. Ibid., p. 93.

4. Goldstein 1989, pp. 391–392.

5. Rupen 1979, p. 46.

6. Ya 1994, pp. 417–418.

7. Goldstein 1989, p. 625.

8. Ibid., p. 626.

9. Shikang (Xigang) province was created in 1927 out of ethnographic Tibetan areas that now comprise western Sichuan province. It was incorporated into Sichuan province in 1955.

10. Ibid., pp. 628–629.

11. Ibid., p. 630. By contrast, President Truman ordered the U.S. 7th Fleet to begin patrolling the Taiwan Straits in June 1950 to demonstrate U.S. commitment to the security of Taiwan (Harding 1992).

12. Mao 1977.

13. In 1949–50, China was divided (by the Chinese Communists) into four large military-civil bureaus. These were charged with operating newly liberated areas until a time when "people's governments" could be established. The S.W. Bureau was in charge of Yunnan, Sichuan, Guizhou, and Tibet.

14. Goldstein 1989, p. 715.

15. So did the United States.

16. India also argued that bringing up the Tibet issue at that time would hurt its efforts to achieve a ceasefire in Korea.

17. Claims that this agreement is invalid since it was signed under duress are misleading. Certainly the Tibetans did not want to sign a treaty acknowledging Chinese sovereignty, but like many defeated countries had little choice. The Chinese negotiators on several occasions made threats to continue the invasion into Central Tibet if certain points were not accepted, but the Tibetan negotiators were never

themselves physically threatened and were free to refuse to sign an agreement right up to the end. Similarly, the common charge that the seal of the Tibetan government was forged by the Chinese is incorrect. The Chinese made only personal seals for each of the Tibetan delegates and these are what they used to sign the agreement. See Goldstein 1989, chap. 20, for a detailed discussion of this agreement.

18. Goldstein 1989, p. 765.

19. Ibid., pp. 763–769. The Common Programme was the 1949 precursor to China's constitution.

20. Ibid., pp. 759–760.

21. The development of U.S. involvement is discussed in detail in Goldstein 1989, p. 763 ff.

22. Goldstein 1989 , p. 794.

23. Cited in Goldstein 1989, p. 798.

24. Dalai Lama, interview with Goldstein, April, 1995.

25. The author is currently completing a book-length monograph on Sino-Tibetan relations during the 1950s.

26. Dalai Lama, interview with Goldstein, April, 1995.

27. It is interesting to note that this was taking place while Mao was turning more leftist in China proper, launching the antirightist campaign in 1957 and the Great Leap Forward in 1958.

28. Immediately after the 1959 uprising, monasteries were classified according to degree of involvement in the uprising. In those designated as "involved," most monks were either sent home or sent to work units (as laymen). A few monasteries not involved in the uprising such as Tashilhunpo, the seat of the Panchen Lama, continued to function as monasteries until the Cultural Revolution. In other important monasteries, a small number of monks were permitted to remain to look after their possessions, etc. The well-known destruction of monastic buildings, books, statues, and so forth mainly occurred a few years later during the Cultural Revolution in 1966–67.

29. It should be noted that Deng Xiaoping was intimately involved in the Tibet Question. From 1949 to 1955 he was political commissar of the S.W. Bureau in Chongqing (which was in charge of the 1950 invasion and administration of Tibet). He moved to Beijing in 1955 where he served as general secretary of the party.

30. UN Resolution 1723 (XVI) of December 20, 1961, cited in Van Pragg 1987.

31. International Commission of Jurists 1959, p. iv.

32. Public Records Office (FO371 150710), Feb. 20, 1960, letter from Christian A. Herter to the Dalai Lama.

33. Memorandum from Assistant Secretary of State for Far Eastern Affairs (Parsons) to Secretary of State Herter, October 14, 1959 (cited in *Foreign Relations of the United States, 1958–60, vol. 19, China.*

34. And presumably an indeterminate number of Tibetans in Tibet.

35. Goldstein, Siebenschuh, and Tsering 1997, p. 108.

36. Ibid. pp. 109–110.

37. Goldstein and Beall 1990, pp. 40–46.

THE POST–MAO ERA

1. *Tibetan Review,* June 1978, p. 4.; Feb. 1979, p. 9ff.; Feb 1989, p. 9. Deng Xiaoping had also raised the Tibetan Question on December 28, 1978 when he responded to U.S. journalists that "the Dalai Lama may return, but only as a citizen of China." And, "we have but one demand—patriotism. And we say that anyone is welcome, whether he embraces patriotism early or late." Deng added that even though the Dalai Lama disliked the government in the past, if he now likes it, the past is irrelevant. (*Ren min Ribau* [*People's Daily,* Beijing edition], "White Paper," 9/24/92).

2. Goldstein 1990.

3. From the "Report of the National United Front Work Conference," 23 January 1982, (Minzu zhengce wenxuan, *Selected Documents of Nationality Policy.* Urumqi: Xinjiang renmin chuban she, 1985, p. 10), as cited in Sharlho 1992, p. 38.

4. National here refers to nationality or ethnic.

5. *Summary of World Broadcasts.* 30 May 1980 (NCNA in Chinese).

6. In China there are no "nationality" Communist parties. Consequently, the Communist party in Tibet is part of the one undivided Chinese Communist Party (CCP), and is subordinate to its policies.

7. It should be noted that the Han cadre withdrawal policy ran into many obstacles in Tibet because disapproving "leftist" cadre dragged their feet in implementation and because many of these Han cadre decided it was in their economic self-interest to remain in Tibet. Generally, the Chinese officials with special skills such as doctors, scientists, and so forth were eager to leave because they had no trouble finding suitable work, but those without such skills quickly found that they were worse off in the other areas of China. The central government had stipulated that their home province had to accept them, but had not stipulated that this acceptance would be at the same

salary and with equivalent perks. These officials also had their families with them in Lhasa, most of whom were earning income. When they came to realize that returning to inland China would mean a drop in their standard of living, a large number protested and insisted that the salary/perks issue be decided in advance, i.e., before they left Tibet. As a result of these issues, the withdrawal policy was never fully implemented. In fact, it probably had the unintended consequence of encouraging the best, most skilled cadre to leave and the least skilled to remain.

8. *News Tibet*. September–December, 1993, p. 7.; and a ms., *Office of Tibet*.

9. *Beijing Review* 49 (5): 10, 1984.

10. *Tibetan Review* (May 1983): 5.

11. In October 1982, e.g., the Office of Tibet in New York City submitted a fourteen-page document on "Chinese Human Rights Abuses in Tibet: 1959–1982."

12. One scholar (Dawa Norbu 1991) has written that the exiles raised these points at the 1982 meeting, but that appears to be incorrect.

13. The new strategy was finalized, it appears, after a series of high-level meetings between key Tibetan and Western supporters in New York, Washington, and London in 1986/87. The history of these developments has not yet been well-documented and details are still sparse.

14. In fact, he first visited the United States only in 1979, having previously been denied a visa for ten years (Grunfeld, unpublished manuscript).

15. *News Tibet* 22 (3) May/August 1988, p. 8. The exiled Tibetans had received their first explicit support from the U.S. Congress in July, 1985, when ninety-one members of congress signed a letter to Li Xiannian, president of the PRC, expressing support for continued direct talks and urging the Chinese to "grant the very reasonable and justified aspirations of His Holiness the Dalai Lama and his people every consideration." (Point 14 of Section 1243 of Foreign Relations Authorization Act, Fiscal Years 1988 and 1989 cited in U.S. Government Printing Office 1992.

16. The talk used "Greater Tibet" as the referent for "Tibet."

17. U.S. Government Printing Office 1992, p. 96.

18. Ibid.

19. Much of this and the next section was adapted from Goldstein 1990.

20. This is the collective prayer assembly that was founded by Tsongkapa in 1408. It was banned at the start of the Cultural Revolution and had just been revived in 1986.

21. All but one of these were eventually released before the Prayer Festival started.

22. Other accounts of these events are found in Sharlho 1992 and Schwartz 1994.

23. *Tibet Briefing*, The Office of Tibet, New York City, 1994, p. 24.

24. It was strongly criticized, for example, by the Tibetan Youth Congress, the European Tibetan Youth Association, and the elder brother of the Dalai Lama, Thupten Norbu, who sent a letter to Tibetans throughout the world attacking his brother's decision to relinquish the goal of independence. However, informed sources in Dharamsala say that the head of the Tibetan Youth Congress publically stated at a meeting at which he was being attacked for criticizing the Dalai Lama, that it was the Dalai Lama who asked him to take the hard-line stand, presumably so he could gracefully pull back from the terms he had just announced.

25. "Tibet—Its Ownership and Human Rights Situation." *Beijing Review* (September 28–October 4 1992): 22.

26. The Dalai Lama's Department of Information and International Relations states in a background report that the Dalai Lama offered to send a ten-member religious delegation to participate. (*World Tibet News* 30 Nov. 1995.)

27. *Beijing Review*, August 8–14, 1994. International Campaign for Tibet, 2/11/1994.

28. They are, therefore, coming not on orders from Beijing but because there are lucrative jobs to be had and money to be earned.

29. One is reminded of the difficulties indigenous populations in Malaysia and Indonesia faced trying to compete with resident Chinese.

30. Comment of Deng Xiaoping to Jimmy Carter, *Tibet Daily* (Ch. edition), 22 November 1993 (the comment was made on 29 June 1987).

31. Since Beijing does not have to worry about votes for its policy in Tibet, this is not a constituency in the normal Western sense. It resembles more the "facts on the ground" type of constituency that Israel uses on the West Bank, although these "facts" do not have citizenship in Tibet.

32. The very fact that Tibetan cadre were doing this illustrates the magnitude of Beijing's problem.

33. *Tibet Information Network Update* (1355–3313), May 6, 1997.

THE FUTURE

1. Although the golden urn lottery had been used on a number of occasions after 1792, it was not used for the last two Dalai Lamas or the last Panchen Lama.

2. The late Panchen Lama in 1988 wrote why he couldn't return to Tibet in 1949, "The Kashag (the Tibetan local government in Lhasa) had not recognized me as Panchen, so I couldn't go to Tibet. (According to Tibetan tradition, the confirmation of either the Dalai or the Panchen must be mutually recognized.)" (Panchen Lama 1988, p. 11.)

3. *Tibet Press Watch*, May 1995, p. 13, and Gyalo Thondup, comments made to delegation of National Committee on U.S. China Relations, November 1995, Hong Kong.

4. Gyalo Thondup was in Beijing as part of a secret delegation sent by the Dalai Lama. They carried letters to Deng Xiaoping and Jiang Zemin (see Dalai Lama 1993).

5. Gyalo Thondup, comments made to delegation of National Committee on U.S. China Relations, November 1995, Hong Kong.

6. Ibid.

7. FBIS—CHI-95-229, 29 November 1995, from Xinhua.

8. Apropos of this, R. Barnett (personal communication, April 1997) indicated that the Dalai Lama had already worked with a BBC film crew doing a piece on the selection of the Panchen Lama, creating incontrovertible film evidence that he had done the confirming divination before the Chinese announcement so there would be evidence that he had actually confirmed the boy before the Chinese. This could have been used as a face-saving device among his followers in exile.

9. These taxes were primarily to pay for the expansion of the army.

10. The Regulations of 1792 began the custom of the Chinese-run golden urn lottery.

11. The decree stated there was no need for "confirmation formalities" (i.e., the golden urn lottery).

12. Ya 1994, pp. 309–312.

13. Ya 1994, pp. 337–338.

14. However, as mentioned earlier, Mao did not want to elevate the Panchen Lama to political equality with the Dalai Lama, so he rejected the proposal to treat the Panchen Lama as head of a "Back Tibet" centered on Tashilhunpo that was equal to the Dalai Lama's "Front Tibet" centered on Lhasa.

15. FBIS—CHI-95-229, 29 November 1995, from Xinhua; FBIS—CHI-95-223, 4 November 1995, from Lhasa Radio.

16. FBIS—CHI-95-223, Lhasa Radio Broadcast, 3 November 1995.

17. *Tibet Press Watch*, May 1995, p. 13.

18. Xinhua News Agency, May 7, 1997, cited in *World Tibet News*.

19. The source for this is a senior Tibetan exile official.

20. Copy of letter dated February 21, 1997, provided by the International Campaign for Tibet.

21. Reuters, 20 January 1997.

22. Reuters, Taipei, 27 March 1997.

23. Internal unity among the exiles has been shaken over the past few years as a result of the Dalai Lama's willingness to forsake complete independence, and as a result of his prohibition of the worship of a Yellow Hat sect protector deity called Shungden. Threats have been made against the Dalai Lama's life, and in February 1997, a key monastic official working for the Dalai Lama was assassinated in Dharamsala by Tibetan dissidents.

24. Actually, in a recent TV interview, the Dalai Lama responded to a question about Buddhism and violence with the intriguing response that "intentions" are more important than actions, and that if acts, even violent ones, are carried out with pure intentions, they would not be evil.

25. *Tibet Information Network* News Update, 28 December 1996, SSN 1355–3313.

26. The first "official" U.S.–Tibet contact appears to have taken place in 1908 when W. W. Rockhill, President T. Roosevelt's envoy to China, met the thirteenth Dalai Lama. (See Rowland 1967, pp. 36–37.)

27. The U.S. CIA had informed the Tibetan guerrillas by the late 1960s that they were terminating U.S. financial support.

28. Most of the support groups appear to have developed as an outgrowth of the first riots in Lhasa in 1987/88 (see McLaren, forthcoming). An interesting account of the place of Tibet in the Western imagination is found in Bishop 1989.

29. *Tibet Press Watch*. May 1994, p. 5.

30. *Tibet Press Watch*. October 1996, p. 5.

31. President Bush, however, is said to have frankly told the Dalai Lama that he was limited in what the U.S. could do to help Tibet.

32. *Tibet Press Watch*. 1991, vol. 3 (1): 17. The president has the option of commenting on these provisions to clarify the official U.S. position but chose not to, apparently to avoid irritating the pro-Tibet lobby in Congress.

33. *Herald Tribune,* 22 November, 1993, p. 1.

34. An article by Shimuzu (1996) cogently examines the Clinton Administration's China policy.

35. State Department 1995, p. 4.

36. Ibid., p. 1.

37. *World Tibet News,* 11 April 1997 (press release from the Danish Tibet Support Group).

38. *The New York Times,* 16 April 1997, p. 6.

39. One is reminded of the fates of three other "Tibetan areas"— Sikkim, Ladakh, and Bhutan—all of whom, with different degrees of success, had to accommodate the interests of their powerful neighbor, India.

40. He would also have to agree to the legitimacy of the Panchen Lama chosen in China. However, since a lama like the late Panchen Lama can decide to incarnate into several new bodies simultaneously, it is possible to have two incarnations of one lama and this should pose no insurmountable problem.

Bibliography

Bell, Charles. 1946. *Portrait of the Dalai Lama*. London: Collins.

Bishop, Peter. 1989. *The Myth of Shangri-La*. Berkeley: University of California Press.

Dawa Norbu. 1991. "China's Dialogue with the Dalai Lama, 1987–90: Pre-negotiation State or Dead End?" *Pacific Affairs* 64 (3).

De Filippi, Filippo (ed.). 1937. *An Account of Tibet: The Travels of Ippolito Desideri of Pistoia, S.J., 1712–1727*. London: Routledge and Sons.

Dung dkar, Blo bzang 'phrin las. 1983. *Bod kyi chos srid zung 'brel skor bshad pa* [Concerning Tibet's joint religious-secular (system)]. Beijing: Nationalities Publishing House.

Gehyelpa Tenzin Dorje. 1989. "The Organization of the Original Tibetan Local Government." *Tibet Studies* (2): 223–230.

Goldstein, Melvyn C. 1989. *A History of Modern Tibet, 1913–1951: The Demise of the Lamaist State*. Berkeley: University of California Press.

———. 1990. "The Dragon and the Snow Lion: The Tibet Question." In Anthony J. Kane (ed.), *China Briefing*. Boulder: Westview Press.

Goldstein, Melvyn C., and Cynthia M. Beall. 1990. *Nomads of Western Tibet: The Survival of a Way of Life*. Berkeley: University of California Press.

Goldstein, Melvyn, William Siebenschuh, and Tashi Tsering. 1997. *The Search for Modern Tibet: The Autobiography of Tashi Tsering*. Armonk, N.Y.: M. E. Sharpe.

Grasso, June, Jay Corin, and Michael Kort. 1991. *Modernization and Revolution in China*. Armonk, N.Y.: M. E. Sharpe.

Grunfeld, Tom A. "The Internationalization of Tibet." Unpublished manuscript.

Harding, Henry. 1992. *A Fragile Relationship: The United States and China since 1972*. Washington, D.C.: The Brookings Institution.

International Commission of Jurists. 1959. *The Question of Tibet and the Rule of Law*. Geneva: International Commission of Jurists.

Kolmas, Josef. 1967. *Tibet and Imperial China: A Survey of Sino-Tibetan Relations up to the End of the Manchu Dynasty in 1912.* Occasional Paper 7. Canberra: The Australian National University, Centre of Oriental Studies.

Lamb, Alastair. 1960. *Britain and Chinese Central Asia: The Road to Lhasa, 1767–1905.* London: Routledge and Kegan Paul.

———. 1966. *The McMahon Line, 1904–1914.* London: Routledge and Kegan Paul.

———. 1989. *Tibet, China and India, 1915–1950: A History of Imperial Diplomacy.* N.p.: Roxford Books.

Li, Tieh-Tseng. 1960. *Tibet: Today and Yesterday.* New York: Bookman Associates.

Mao Zedung. 1977. *Ma'o tse tung gi gsung rtsom gces bsdus* (Mao's collected works), vol. 5.

McLaren, Meg. Forthcoming. "Computing for Tibet. Virtual Politics in the Post–Cold War Era." In G. Marcus (ed.), *Late Editions,* vol. 3. Chicago: University of Chicago Press.

Moynihan, Daniel P. 1994. *Pandaemonium: Ethnicity in International Politics.* Oxford: Oxford University Press.

Office of Tibet. 1990. *Tibet Briefing.* New York: Office of Tibet.

Panchen Lama. 1988. "On Tibetan Independence." *China Reconstructs* (January): 10–11.

Phuntso Tashi. 1995. *Mi tshe'i byung ba brjod pa.* [My life story]. Dharamsala: Library of Tibetan Works and Archives.

Richardson, Hugh E. 1984. *Tibet and Its History.* Boulder: Shambhala.

———. 1985. *A Corpus of Early Tibetan Inscriptions.* London: Royal Asiatic Society.

Rong, Ma, and Pan Naigu. 1994. "The Tibetan Population and Their Geographic Distribution in China." In P. Kvaerne (ed.), *Tibetan Studies: Proceedings of the 6th Seminar of the International Association for Tibetan Studies, Fagernes, 1992,* vol. 1, Oslo: Institute for Comparative Research in Human Culture.

Rossabi, Morris. 1988. *Kublai Khan: His Life and Times.* Berkeley: University of California Press.

Rowland, W. 1967. "American Diplomacy and the God King." *Foreign Service Journal.*

Rupen, Robert. 1979. *How Mongolia Is Really Ruled.* Stanford: Hoover Institution Press.

Schwartz, Ronald D. 1994. *Circle of Protest: Political Ritual in the Tibetan Uprising.* New York: Columbia University Press.

Shakabpa, Tsepon W. D. 1967. *Tibet: A Political History.* New Haven: Yale University Press.

Shakya, Tsering. 1995. "The Greater Significance of the Panchen Lama Dispute." *Tibetan Review* 30 (8): 14–18.

Sharlho, T. W. 1992. "China's Reforms in Tibet: Issues and Dilemmas." *Journal of Contemporary China* 1 (1): 34–60.

Shimuzu, Yoshikazu. 1996. "The Clinton Administration's Failed China Policy: Implications of U.S.–China Negotiations over MFN and Human Rights." *East Asian Institute Reports.* New York: East Asian Institute, Columbia University.

Snellgrove, David, and Hugh Richardson. 1980. *A Cultural History of Tibet.* Boulder: Prajna Press.

State Department. 1995. *Relations of the United States with Tibet.* Washington, D.C.: State Department of the United States.

Teichman, Eric. 1922. *Travels of a Consular Officer in Eastern Tibet.* Cambridge: Cambridge University Press.

U.S. Government Printing Office. 1992. *Congressional Ceremony to Welcome His Holiness the Dalai Lama of Tibet.* Washington, D.C.:

Van Pragg, Michael. 1987. *The Status of Tibet.* Boulder: Westview Press.

Ya, Hanzhang. 1991 *The Biographies of the Dalai Lamas.* Beijing: Foreign Language Press.

———. 1994. *Biographies of the Tibetan Spiritual Leaders Panchen Erdenis.* Beijing: Foreign Language Press.

Index

Compositor: Publication Services, Inc.
Text: 10/13 Palatino
Display: Centaur
Printer: Maple-Vail Book Manufacturing Group
Binder: Maple-Vail Book Manufacturing Group